A LO

THE FIVE MAFIA FAMILIES

OF NEW YORK CITY

Written By

David Pietras
All Rights Reserved
© 2013

Copyright © 2013 by David J. Pietras

http://mrdavepp.wix.com/davidpietras

Cover design by David Pietras

ISBN-13: 978-1494797249

ISBN-10: 1494797240

1 2 3 4 5 6 7 8 9 10 13

Prologue

From Gotti to Gigante, the names atop today's Mafia organizational charts are old ones. But the times have certainly changed for New York's biggest families—and not for the better. In this book we will look at New York City's Five Families. All have bookmaking, loan-sharking, and extortion rackets. The Genovese family and, to a lesser degree, the Lucchese family (like the Gambinos) also have viable labor-racketeering endeavors that let them invest and launder their ill-gotten gains in "legitimate" industries. Every Family has declined as of late, some more than others.

So you want to know all about the **New York Mafia Families**, uh?

If we are going to talk about the New York Mafia, then we must learn about "The Commission" First.

The Mafia Commission

The Commission is the governing body of the Mafia in the US. It has changed a lot since it was created in 1931 but the bosses of the New York Five Mafia Families still are the core membership of The Commission.

The Commission was created in '31 by Lucky (Luciano, of course) in Atlantic City. Its purpose was to replace the old Sicilian mafia regime and establish some ground rules among the new mafia families. Historically, a system like this has always been in place. In Sicily, the heads of each *cosche* would meet regularly to discuss "business", and in the US, they wouldn't forget their traditions.

In the beginning of 1931, after winning a bloody War among the New York gangs, the New York Boss Salvatore Maranzano divided all the gangs in the US into several mafia families and then he assumed as *capo di tutti capi* ("boss of all bosses"). Because there had never been a "boss of all bosses" in the Mafia History, the mafia's ranks reacted negatively to this. Luciano, who was by then a Maranzano ally, soon abraded under the harsh control by

Maranzano and in September of that year he machined Maranzano's assassination. Luciano then became the top mobster in the country.

Salvatore Maranzano

Joseph C. Bonanno came to power in 1931 with the assassination of Sicilian-born Mafia boss Salvatore Maranzano in New York in the culmination of the legendary Castellammarese War, which marked the beginning of the modern age of organized crime in America. Just five months earlier Maranzano had wrested the top slot from Giuseppe Joe the Boss Masseria, the old-fashioned Mustache Pete who had ruled the Italian-American gangs in New York City with an iron fist. Masseria had been gunned down one spring afternoon at his favorite Coney Island restaurant. Maranzano was slightly more forward thinking that Masseria, but to the young Turks champing at the bit to do things their way, he was just another Mustache Pete who needed to be replaced. Charles Lucky Luciano, who had been Masseria's second in command, was the prime architect of the plan to overthrow all the old-timers.

Joseph Bonanno in his autobiography, *A Man of Honor,* claims that he knew nothing of the plot to kill Maranzano, a statement that defies mob logic. If he had been as loyal to Maranzano as he says, then he too would have been assassinated. But in fact he benefited greatly from Maranzano's demise, becoming the boss of a sizeable portion of Maranzano's gang. At age 26, he became the youngest crime boss in America.

Since then, gang wars didn't "stopped" but they did reduce its scale and frequency.

The current Known Bosses of the Mafia Commission are:

Bonanno Crime Family – Unknown

Colombo Crime Family – Andrew "Andy Mush" Russo

Gambino Crime Family – Daniel "Danny" Marino/Giovanni "Johnny" Gambino/Robert "Bobby" Vernace

Genovese Crime Family – Unknown

Lucchese Crime Family – Steven "Wonderboy" Crea/Aneillo "Neil" Migliore/Joseph "Joey Dee" DiNapoli

Now that we know how it all began, we can move on to really understand the **New York Mafia**.

Fictional portrayals:

The Commission has been depicted in a few Hollywood films, primarily in "The Godfather" and "The Godfather III".

The Five Families:

The Five Families refers to the five major Italian-American Mafia families that have dominated New York City's underworld since 1930. The Five Mafia Families of New York remain as the main powerhouse of the Sicilian Mafia in the United States.

The Current Five Mafia Families Bosses:

Bonanno: Vincent "Vinny Gorgeous" Basciano (Salvatore Montagna is the acting boss)

Gambino: (Ruling Committee/Panel – Daniel "Danny" Marino, Giovanni "Johnny" Gambino, Robert "Bobby" Vernace)

Colombo: Carmine "Junior" Persico (Thomas Gioeli is the acting boss)

Genovese: Unknown Boss (Daniel Leo is the acting boss)

Lucchese: Vittorio "Vic" Amuso (Ruling Committee/Panel – Aniello "Neil" Migliore, Joseph "Joey Dee" DiNapoli, Matthew Madonna)

Fictional portrayals
and Curious Facts:

As we mentioned before, the Five Families' Commission was depicted in *The Godfather* series. What you may not know is that the famous "The Sopranos" TV series DiMeo Family of NJ has close business connections with the Lupertazzi Mafia Family of Brooklyn, one of the five families in New York. Members of the DeCavalcante family believed themselves to be the inspiration for the DiMeo family.

So, now that you have the breakdown on The Commission let's take a look at each one of the Families.

Bonanno crime family

The **Bonanno crime family** is one of the "Five Families" that dominates organized crime activities in New York City, within the nationwide criminal phenomenon known as the American Mafia (or *Cosa Nostra*).

Joseph Bonanno

Founded and named after Joseph Bonanno, for over 30 years the family was one of the most powerful in the country. However, in the early 1960's, Bonanno attempted to seize the mantle of boss of bosses, but failed and was forced to retire. This touched off a period of turmoil within the family that lasted almost a quarter-century. It was the first of the New York families to be kicked off the Commission (a council of the bosses that helps to maintain order in the Mafia), due to infighting for the boss's mantle and allegations the family was actively dealing heroin. Later, the family faced shaky leadership, with the acting boss Carmine Galante murdered in 1979 at the command of Philip Rastelli, the actual boss. The family only recovered in the 1990s under Joseph Massino, and by the dawn of the new millennium was not only back on the Commission, but was the most powerful family in New York. There were also two major setbacks: in 1981, they learned that an FBI agent named Joe Pistone, calling himself Donnie Brasco had infiltrated their ranks; and in 2004, a rash of convictions and defections culminated in Massino becoming a government informant.

Joseph D. Pistone

FBI surveillance photo of Donnie Brasco

Let's take a look at the history back to the Sicilian origins.

The origins of the Bonanno crime family can be traced back to the town of Castellammare del Golfo located in the Province of Trapani, Sicily. The Bonanno Mafia clan was led by boss Giuseppe "Peppe" Bonanno and his older brother Stefano as advisor. The strongest ally of the Bonanno clan was the boss of the Magaddino Mafia clan Stefano Magaddino. During the 1900s, the Bonanno and Magaddino Mafia clans feuded with Felice Buccellato, the boss of the Buccellato Mafia clan. After the deaths of Stefano Bonanno and Giuseppe Bonanno the youngest of the Bonanno brothers Salvatore took revenge, killing members of the Buccellato clan. In 1903, Salvatore Bonanno married Catherine Bonventre and on January 18, 1905 she gave birth to Giuseppe. Three years later Salvatore Bonanno moved his family to New York City. While away Stefano Magaddino took over running the Bonanno-Magaddino-Bonventre Mafia clan. Salvatore Bonanno along with members of the Bonanno-Magaddino-Bonventre clan began establishing dominance and control in the Castellammarese community of Williamsburg, Brooklyn. While operating in Brooklyn, the Castellammarese leaders were able to preserve the criminal organization's future. In 1911, Salvatore Bonanno returned to Sicily and died of a heart attack in 1915. Stefano Magaddino arrived in New York and became a powerful member of the Castellammarese clan. In 1921, Magaddino fled to Buffalo to avoid murder charges. The Castellammarese clan was taken over by Nicola Schirò.

Castellammarese War

In 1927, violence broke out between the two rival New York Mafia factions and soon developed into a full out war known as the Castellammarese War. The conflict started when members of the Castellammarese clan began hijacking truckloads of illegal liquor that belonged to Giuseppe "Joe the Boss" Masseria. The Castellammarese clan was based in Williamsburg, Brooklyn and led by Nicola "Cola" Schirò who tried to work with Masseria. But one of the group's leaders Salvatore Maranzano wanted to take control over New York's underworld. Maranzano took control of the Castellammarese clan continuing a bloody Mafia War.

The Castellammarese faction was more organized and unified than Masseria family. Maranzano's allies were Buffalo family Boss Stefano Magaddino, Detroit family Boss Gaspar Milazzo and Philadelphia family Boss Salvatore Sabella, all Castellammarese. Maranzano's faction included mobsters Joseph Bonanno, Carmine Galante, and Gaspar DiGregorio. Maranzano was also close to Joseph Profaci future boss of the New York Profaci family. Finally, Maranzano established a secret alliance with Bronx Reina family Boss Gaetano Reina, a nominal Masseria ally.

After Reina's murder on February 26, 1930, members of the Masseria faction began to defect to Maranzano. By 1931, momentum had shifted to Castellammarese faction. That spring, a group of younger Mafiosi from both camps, known as the "Young Turks", decided to switch to Maranzano and end the war. This group included future mob bosses Charles "Lucky" Luciano, Vito Genovese, Frank Costello, Tommy Lucchese, Albert Anastasia and

Joe Adonis. As leader of the Young Turks, Luciano concluded a secret deal with Maranzano and promised to kill Masseria. On April 15, 1931 Masseria was murdered ending the long Castellammarese War.

Maranzano's murder and The Commission

After Masseria's death, Maranzano outlined a peace plan to all the Sicilian and Italian Mafia leaders in the United States. There would be 24 organizations (to be known as "families") throughout the United States who would elect their own *boss*. In New York City, Maranzano established five Cosa Nostra families: the Luciano family under Lucky Luciano, the Mangano family under Vincent Mangano, the Gagliano family under Tommy Gagliano, the Profaci family under Joseph Profaci, and the Maranzano crime family under himself. Maranzano created an additional post for himself, that of *capo di tutti capi*, or Boss of Bosses.

Although Maranzano was more forward-looking than Masseria, at bottom he was still a Mustache Pete. It did not take long for Maranzano and Luciano to come into conflict. Luciano was not pleased that Maranzano had reneged on his promise of equality, and soon came to believe he was even more hidebound and greedy that Masseria had been. Maranzano, in turn, grew uncomfortable with Luciano's ambitions and opposed his partnership with Jewish mobsters Meyer Lansky and Bugsy Siegel. Maranzano secretly plotted to have Luciano killed. However, after Lucchese alerted Luciano that he was marked for death, Luciano struck first on September 10, 1931. Jewish gangsters hired by Luciano murdered Maranzano in his office. Now in control of the Cosa Nostra, Luciano replaced the "Boss of Bosses" with The Commission to regulate the Mafia's national affairs and mediate disputes between families. Luciano was appointed the first chairman of the Commission.

The Bonanno era

After Maranzano's death, Bonanno was awarded most of Maranzano's crime family. At only 26 years old, Bonanno was the youngest Mafia leader in the nation. Years later, he claimed not to have known about the plot to eliminate Maranzano, but it is very unlikely that Luciano would have allowed him to live had he still backed Maranzano. Bonanno directed his family into illegal gambling, loansharking, and narcotics. The family also built significant criminal interests in California and Arizona. With the support of his cousin, Buffalo crime family boss Stefano Magaddino, Bonanno also expanded into Canada.

Like Maranzano, Bonanno believed in the Old World Mafia traditions of "honor", "tradition", "respect" and "dignity" as principles for ruling his family. He was more steeped in these traditions than other mobsters of his generation. The Bonanno family was considered the closest knit of the Five Families because Bonanno tried to restrict membership to Castellammarese Sicilians. He strongly believed that blood relations and a strict Sicilian upbringing would be the only way to hold the traditional values of the Mafia together.

Over the years, Bonanno became a powerful member of the Commission due to his close relationship with fellow boss Joe Profaci. In 1956, the relationship between the two bosses became stronger when Bonanno's son Salvatore "Bill" Bonanno married Profaci's niece Rosalie. The Bonanno-Profaci alliance deterred the other three families from trying to steal their rackets.

The Bonanno War

(1964-1969)

The stable power relationship between the families collapsed with the death of Joe Profaci in 1962. Bonanno was now threatened by an alliance of Tommy Lucchese and new boss Carlo Gambino. At the same time, Bonanno was facing rising discontent within his own family. In the early 1960's many of the Bonanno family members were complaining that Bonanno spent too much time at his second home in Tucson, Arizona.

In 1963, Bonanno and Joe Magliocco, Profaci's successor as boss of the Profaci family, conspired to wipe out several other mob leaders, Stefano Magaddino, Carlo Gambino, Tommy Lucchese and Frank DeSimone. Magliocco was given the task of wiping out Gambino and Lucchese, and gave the contract to one of his top hit men, Joe Colombo. However, Colombo instead alerted Gambino and Lucchese. The other bosses quickly realized that Magliocco could not possibly have planned this by himself. Knowing how close the Bonanno and Profaci families had been over the last three decades, they viewed Bonanno as the real mastermind. The commission summoned Magliocco and Bonanno. In view of their pioneering roles in the New York Mafia, the commission intended to go easy on them, with nothing more than a fine and loss of their family. However, only Magliocco showed up. He admitted his role in the plot and was forced to give up his family to Colombo.

"What's There to Say?"

Joseph C. Bonanno

On the evening of October 20, 1964, Joseph Bonanno, the boss of the New York crime family that bore his name, sat down to dinner at an uptown restaurant with three of his attorneys: William Maloney, his partner Joe Allen, and Bonannos Arizona attorney Lawrence DAntonio. The sixty-year-old Bonanno was scheduled to appear before a grand jury the next day, and the lawyers had assembled to counsel him. Bonanno would later refer to this time of his life as being between a hammer and anvil. The federal government was actively pursuing him for his organized-crime activities while at the same time the Mafia Commission, the mobs ruling body in America, had gotten wind of his plans to revamp their ranks through a series of planned assassinations in order to make himself boss of all bosses.

Charles "Lucky" Luciano

Bonanno felt he deserved the vaunted position since in his estimation he, unlike his so-called peers, was the only remaining man of honor in the tradition of the Sicilian Mafia. Wealth, he would later write in his controversial 1983 autobiography, was a by-product of power. According to Bonanno, Lucky Luciano and his ilk concerned themselves with the most primitive consideration: making money-an interesting statement coming from a man whose crime family made most of its profits from the sale and distribution of narcotics. During his unprecedented 33 year reign, Bonanno used his considerable ill-gotten gain to extend his empire beyond the New York City area, acquiring major interests in Arizona, California, Canada, Cuba, and Haiti.

The boss and his lawyers lingered long after their meal was over that night and finally left the restaurant close to midnight. They flipped up their overcoat collars against a steady drizzle as they flagged down a taxi. Bonanno, Maloney, and Allen got in, and Maloney told the driver to go to his apartment building at 36th Street and Park Avenue where they planned to continue their conference. Bonanno had been invited to stay at Maloney's apartment that night, so he wouldn't have to commute into Manhattan from his Long Island home for the next day's hearing. In his autobiography, Bonanno says that although he knew he was in hot water, he didn't fear for his life and traveled without a bodyguard.

When the taxi pulled up at the curb in front of Maloney's apartment, Allen got out first and walked to the canopy at the entrance to get out of the rain while Bonanno and Maloney argued over who would pay the fare. Bonanno insisted, and Maloney conceded, following his partner to the canopy as their client paid the driver.

Bonanno stepped onto the sidewalk, closed the door, and the taxi pulled away. He didn't notice the two men walking toward him until they grabbed him by the arms and roughly hustled him toward the corner.

Come on, Joe, one of the men said. My boss wants you.

According Bonannos account, they were tall, had long coats and brimmed hats.

Maloney shouted at them, but a gunshot into the sidewalk at his feet sent him scurrying for shelter.

The two men dragged Bonanno to a waiting car and shoved him in the backseat, ordering him to crouch on the floor...head down. The car sped off, making several sharp turns that jostled the boss. Finally the car stopped turning and picked up speed. Bonanno assumed they were on a highway.

The two men told Bonanno he could sit up now and instructed him to sit between them. Their driver kept his eye on the road, and they started apologizing to Bonanno for having to manhandle him. That's when Bonanno recognized the two sad faces. One was his cousin, Nino Maggadino, brother of Stefano Maggadino, the mob boss of Buffalo. The other man was Stefano's son Peter.

Cosa si puo dire? Peter said to his uncle Joe in Sicilian-accented Italian. What's there to say?

Bonanno said nothing. He knew why his cousin Stefano had ordered this kidnapping. Bonanno had put out a contract on Stefano Maggadino's life, but the plot had been revealed and thwarted. Obviously this was Maggadino's retaliation.

The cars headlights swept the curving entrance ramp that led to the George Washington Bridge. Through the car windows, Bonanno could see the shimmering waters of the Hudson River and the brightly lit Manhattan skyline to his left as they made their way to New Jersey.

On October 21, Bonanno disappeared and wasn't heard from again for almost two years. After months of no word from Bonanno the Commission named capo Gaspar DiGregorio the new boss. Gaspar "Gasparino" DiGregorio The family split into two factions, the *DiGregorio supporters* and the *Bonanno loyalists*. In the media the event was referred to as the *"Banana Split"* or *"Banana War"*. The *Bonanno loyalists* were led by Bonanno's brother-in-law Frank Labruzzo and his son Bill Bonanno. In 1966, DiGregorio arranged for a sit-down in a house on Troutman Street in Brooklyn. DiGregorio's men arrived at the meeting, and when Bill Bonanno arrived a large gun battle ensued. The DiGregorio loyalists had planned to wipe out the opposition, but they failed, and no one was killed.

Bonanno had a gift for making money, and unlike the narrow-minded Mustache Petes, he boldly diversified his operations. Under Bonanno, the family raked in profits from gambling, loan-sharking, and narcotics. Interestingly, like *The Godfather*s Don Corleone, Bonanno vociferously condemned drug dealing and denied ever having any part in it, but in fact, as Carl Sifakis states in *The Mafia Encyclopedia,* the Bonanno Family was one of the major suppliers of drugs in New York City. Bonanno also had interests in motels, the garment industry, and a funeral parlor.

Stefano Maggadino

With the sanction of his cousin Stefano Maggadino, the mob boss of Buffalo, Bonanno started rackets in Canada. He claimed Arizona for himself, starting a realty and insurance company in Tucson and buying into a nearby cotton ranch. He edged into California where the local mob families (mockingly known as the Mickey Mouse Mafia) were hardly making a dent. Bonanno also bought into a cheese factory in Wisconsin and owned a 280-acre dairy farm in upstate New York. Bonanno invested in Cuban casinos with Jewish gangster Meyer Lansky and explored Haiti as another possible gambling destination.

Tommy Lucchese

By the early 1960's Bonannos wildly ambitious ventures caused grumbling within the ranks of the family. Many of his soldiers complained that he was neglecting the New York operations in favor of his other holdings. Some of the other New York bosses disapproved of the way he conducted business, but Bonanno considered himself a cut above his peers and the only true man of honor among them. Fortunately for him, his most outrageous impulses were kept in check by his closest ally, Joe Profaci, boss of what would later become known as the Colombo Family. But when Profaci died of cancer in 1962, Bonannos ambitions got the better of him, and he decided to install himself as the rightful boss of all bosses.

He enlisted Profaci's successor, Joe Magliocco, into a plot to assassinate those he felt stood in his way, including prominent New York bosses Carlo Gambino and Tommy Lucchese, Los Angeles boss Frank DeSimone, and Bonannos own cousin, and Buffalo boss Stephano Maggadino.

Joseph Profaci

Bonanno and Magliocco agreed to split the killings with Magliocco taking care of the New York bosses. He gave the assignment to a trusted hitman, Joe Colombo. But when Colombo weighed the odds, he came to the conclusion that Bonanno and Magliocco were the wrong horses to bet on, so instead of carrying out the hits, he informed Lucchese and Gambino of the plot against them. They in turn notified the Mafia Commission.

Joe Colombo

The Commission ordered Bonanno and Magliocco to appear before them and account for themselves. Magliocco obeyed their order and confessed to taking part in the plot. As punishment, the Commission forced him to retire and installed hitman Joe Colombo as his replacement. The Commission could have meted out a harsher sentence, but Magliocco was in poor health and in fact died the next year. The Commission was saving the real retribution for the mastermind of the plot, Bonanno. But instead of facing the music, Bonanno defied them and refused to appear. Furious with his insolence, the Commission dethroned him and declared a disaffected Bonanno Family capo, Gaspar DiGregorio, as the new boss.

With the family now divided into two factions, tensions on the street ran high. The long knives were out for Joe Bonanno, and it was his cousin Stephano Maggadino who got to him first, having him kidnapped. Maggadino held him at an upstate New York farmhouse for six weeks, then had him driven to El Paso, Texas, where Bonanno called a friend in Tucson to come pick him up. Mob expert Jerry

Capeci postulates in *The Complete Idiots Guide to the Mafia* that the entire kidnapping episode was actually an ill-conceived hoax orchestrated by Bonanno himself to avoid testifying before the grand jury in Manhattan. But whether it was real or fabricated, Bonannos disappearance was the spark that ignited what the newspapers would call the Banana War.

The Banana War

With Joe Bonanno missing, the Commission soon lost its patience, probably figuring that they were being played by the elusive boss. They ruled that Bonanno would no longer be considered the head of his family and appointed capo Gaspar DiGregorio the new boss. (DiGregorio had his own beef with Bonanno for earlier denying him the position of family *consigliere,* which he felt he deserved. Instead Bonanno had appointed his own son Bill.) Family members took sides, splitting into two camps, the Bonanno loyalists led by Bill Bonanno and the Commission-backed faction led by DiGregorio.

Harsh words soon led to armed skirmishes on the streets of New York. The other families frowned down on these public outbursts. The Banana War drew unwanted attention to the mob and was ultimately bad for everybody's business. They wanted it stopped. DiGregorio called for a sit-down to put together a peace treaty. Representatives from both sides agreed to meet at a house on Troutman Street in Brooklyn after dark. DiGregorio and his men arrived first, but compromise was not on their minds. As soon as Bill Bonanno showed up, DiGregorio's men opened fire with shotguns and rifles. Bonanno and his men retaliated, shooting into the dark at their unseen assailants. Over 100 rounds were fired, and by some miracle no one died.

Joe Bonanno then offered the Commission a deal to end the violence. He would give up his claim to the family and retire to Arizona if the Commission would accept his son Bill and brother-in-law Frank Labruzzo as boss and underboss.

The Commission saw right through his offer, knowing that Joe Bonanno would remain in control even if he didn't have the title. They came back with a counter offer: Bonanno could retire with his life, but the Commission would name the next boss-DiGregorio.

The war continued. Joe Bonanno resurfaced in May 1966 - 19 months after his alleged kidnapping - then quickly dropped out of sight again. The Commission grew impatient with DiGregorio's ineffective efforts to squelch the Bonanno loyalists, so they replaced him with someone they felt could do the job, Paul Sciacca. But Bonannos men fought like guerillas. Three of Sciacca's men were mowed down by machine-gun fire inside a Queens restaurant. The fighting escalated, and each side lost five more men.

In May 1966, Bonanno reappeared and rallied a large part of the family to his side. He claimed that Magaddino, acting on behalf of the commission, sent two of his soldiers to kidnap Bonanno and held him captive for six weeks. However, this account is almost certainly false based on contemporary accounts of the time. Several of Bonanno's button men were overheard expressing their disgust that Bonanno "took off and left us here alone", and New Jersey crime boss Sam DeCavalcante was overheard saying that Bonanno's disappearance took the other bosses by surprise. Bonanno may have had another reason to disappear—he was facing a subpoena from U.S. Attorney Robert Morgenthau, and faced the choice of either breaking his blood oath or going to jail for contempt. Further peace offers from both sides were spurned with the ongoing violence and murders. The Commission grew tired of the affair and replaced DiGregorio with Paul Sciacca, but the fighting carried on regardless.

Joseph Bonanno

Finally in 1968 Joe Bonanno suffered a major heart attack. He flew to Arizona and informed the Commission that he was retiring, this time for good. The Commission was naturally wary of anything Bonanno did or said, but as time passed, the shootings diminished, and the torn family eventually accepted Sciacca as their leader. He was later succeeded by Natale Evola who was succeeded by Philip Rusty Rastelli.

Natale Evola

Both Joe and Bill Bonanno wrote books about their Mafia experiences. Such public disclosures were serious violations of *omerta,* the Mafia code of silence and especially surprising coming from these self-proclaimed men of honor. It's generally agreed that these tomes paint a picture of the way father and son wished things had been as opposed to way they actually were. The Bonannos also cooperated with author Gay Talese for his book about the crime family, *Honor Thy Father.*

Jerry Capeci in *The Complete Idiots Guide to the Mafia* quotes FBI agent Bill Roemer who had many dealings with Bonanno in Arizona. Roemer called Bonanno a constant whiner who did not live up to the tradition he speaks about so much in his book.

In 2002 Joe Bonanno died of natural causes in Tucson. He
was 97 years old.

The Cigar

Carmine "Lilo" Galante

Carmine Lilo Galante's image of himself might have surpassed even Joe Bonannos. Of course, Galante was Bonannos driver and later his underboss, so he probably heard a lot of self-aggrandizement from the boss, and the attitude apparently rubbed off. But while Bonanno at least publicly tried to take the high road, claiming to be the last man of honor in La Cosa Nostra in America, Galante had no problem getting down and dirty, and he seldom lost a fight.

Vito Genovese

Galante started his criminal career with a bang as a shooter for Vito Genovese, having murdered, among others, Italian journalist and Mussolini critic Carlo Tresca in 1943 on orders from Genovese as a favor to Il Duce. Galante eventually found a place within the ranks of the Bonanno family. He was the kind of aggressive gangster Joe Bonanno needed to break into new rackets in new territories. In 1953 Bonanno put Galante in charge of his Montreal operations where Galante became a top earner for the family, extorting money from other criminals. According to journalist Jerry Capeci, being in Montreal at this time put Galante right in the center of a main transit point for the so-called French Connection. Galante, who earned the nickname the Cigar because he was rarely seen without one in his mouth, got involved in heroin trafficking in a big way despite Joe Bonannos proclamations that his family had nothing to do with narcotics. In 1962, Galante, now the underboss of the family, was convicted on narcotics charges and sentenced to 20 years in prison.

But prison walls did not stop Galante from planning his come-back. His mad-dog ways were well known. In 1931 doctors at Sing Sing Prison had tested him and categorized him as a psychopath while he was serving a stint there, and over the years he more than lived up to that diagnosis. It was no wonder that no one within the Bonanno family-or in any of the other crime families for that matter- looked forward to Galante's eventual release.

Carlo Gambino

Galante had several axes to grind. He felt that he could be a better boss than Bonanno had been. He also despised the Commission members who had forced Joe Bonanno to step down, and Carlo Gambino became the focus of his anger. According to *The Mafia Encyclopedia,* Galante bragged to other inmates at Lewisburg Prison in Pennsylvania that when he got out, he would make Carlo Gambino shit in the middle of Times Square.

Carmine Galante

In 1974 Galante was released from prison after serving 12 years. Despite all his tough talk, he didn't make a move on the ailing Gambino who had a reputation for thinking three steps ahead and outmaneuvering his opponents. Galante did manage to bully Rusty Rastelli into turning over the leadership of the Bonanno family to him. Galante increased the family's involvement in the drug trade, making Montreal their main pipeline for heroin from France. The French Connection flow gushed, and Galante and his associates made millions.

Federal agents arrested Galante in 1978 on a parole violation-associating with known criminals-which tied him up in court, but his attorney Roy Cohn ultimately secured his freedom. By this time Carlo Gambino had passed away, and Galante saw no major obstacles in his way in his quest for total domination of the American Mafia. Drugs were the key to his power because they produced the largest and fastest profits, and he set about to take control of other families narcotics operations.

Eight Genovese Family members involved in the drug trade were gunned down on Galante's orders, and it was clear that the violence wouldn't stop until all mob drug operations were under his thumb.

Santo Trafficante

The other mob bosses felt that Galante was out of line and had to be stopped. At a secret meeting in Boca Raton, Florida, high-ranking representatives from the four other New York families met with Florida boss Santo Trafficante to decide what they would do about Galante. The answer was obvious-he had to go. Mob bosses from all around the country were consulted, including Rusty Rastelli who was in prison and even Joe Bonanno. They all agreed that for the good of La Cosa Nostra, Galante had to die.

Rastelli regime

Mugshot of Carmine Galante in 1943

Due to the infighting of the Bonanno family, it was spurned by the other families and stripped of its Commission seat. Rastelli took charge of a seemingly hapless, doomed organization. Rastelli's former friend Carmine Galante became a powerful and dangerous renegade.

Having previously acted as a focal point for the importation of heroin to the USA via Montreal, Galante set about refining the family's drug trafficking operations. The incredibly lucrative deals he was able to make made the family a fortune, but with the other four families being kept out of the arrangements, Galante was making a rod for his own back.

On July 12, 1979, Galante paid a visit to his favorite restaurant, Joe and Mary's in the Bushwick section of Brooklyn. One of his cousins owned the restaurant, and it was one of the few places where Galante felt he could relax. Galante and a few of his associates took seats in the open-air courtyard behind the restaurant and enjoyed their meal. After the entre, a couple of the men excused themselves to go make phone calls. Galante pulled out a fresh cigar and stuck it in his mouth. But before he could get it lit, three masked men rushed into the courtyard from inside the restaurant, one of them carrying a shotgun. The man quickly squared off and fired both barrels in Galante's chest. The blasts knocked the boss off his chair. He died at the scene, crumpled on the concrete pavement, his blood streaming into a nearby drain, the cigar still in his mouth.

Carmine Galante before and after death

"My Thing"

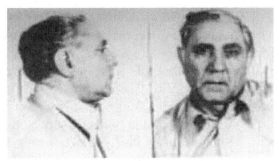

Phillip "Rusty" Rastelli

After the Cigar was snuffed out, Rusty Rastelli returned as boss of the Bonanno Family. According to *The Mafia Encyclopedia,* the family now concentrated on home video pornography, pizza parlors (regarded as an excellent business in which to hide illegal aliens), espresso cafes, restaurants, and a very large narcotics operation. But three of Rastelli's capos Philip Philly Lucky Giaccone, Alphonse Sonny Red Indelicato, and Dominick Big Trin Trinchera-weren't satisfied with their allotted piece of the narcotics pie and pushed for a bigger share. They openly challenged Rastelli's decisions, and before long the family was once again on the verge of splitting into two warring camps.

Rastelli went to the Commission and asked for permission to take care of the problem the old-fashioned way, sending the three rebel capos to an early grave. The Commission refused his request, but then reconsidered when they learned that the trio was planning to overthrow Rastelli.

The contract to take care of the three rebels was given to capo Joseph Massino who organized a hit team largely comprised of shooters from the family's Montreal branch, reasoning that they could escape to Canada as soon as the deed was done. The shooters included Montreal boss Vito Rizzuto and the Sicilian-born capo Gerlando George from Canada Sciascia. Massino lured the three capos to a sit-down at a social club in Bensonhurst, Brooklyn, to supposedly iron out their differences. As soon as everyone was comfortable, four shooters wearing ski masks burst out of a closet and shouted that this was a stickup. As reported on Ganglandnews.com, Vito Rizzuto started the shooting by firing at the largest target, 300-pound Big Trin Trinchera. George from Canada Sciascia shot Sonny Red Indelicato in the head. Lucky Philly Giaccone ran for his life, but Massino pulled his gun and dropped Giaccone before he made it to the door. The shooters left the building immediately, and a second team led by Bonanno capo Dominick Sonny Black Napolitano arrived to supervise the cleanup crew.

These murders, however, did not solve the Bonanno Family's problems. The narcotics trade was just too lucrative to stay away from, and many of Bonanno members flocked to it despite Rastelli's orders. The family was out of control, and with their troublesome history, they lost their seat on the Commission.

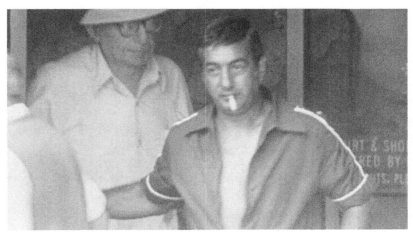

Dominick "Sonny Black" Napolitano

The family's fortunes sank even lower when it was revealed that FBI Special Agent Joseph Pistone had infiltrated their ranks so deeply, he had actually been proposed for full membership. Working undercover as jewel thief Donnie Brasco, Pistone was taken under the wing of soldier Benjamin Lefty Guns Ruggiero who was part of capo Sonny Black Napolitano's crew. Pistone spent six years inside the Bonanno Family. His undercover work and subsequent courtroom testimonies helped win convictions against over 100 wiseguys from crime families across the country. Sonny Black Napolitano paid with his life for letting Donnie Brasco into the Bonanno fold. Juries in New York, Tampa, and Milwaukee found Lefty Guns Ruggiero guilty on a number of charges, which resulted in a twenty-year sentence.

Benjamin "Lefty" Ruggiero

Special Agent Pistone also testified against boss Rusty Rastelli who was convicted on federal RICO charges and sentenced to 12 years in prison. His disastrous reign as boss of the Bonanno Family ended in 1991 when he died of liver cancer in a prison hospital.

Pistone, in his book *Donnie Brasco: My Undercover Life in the Mafia,* sums up the problems that the Bonannos and all the mob families faced as a new generation of gangsters moved up through the ranks. La Cosa Nostra -Our Thing- is becoming My Thing in the hands of the younger generation.

He points to the lure of easy drug profits and drug use by these younger mobsters as corrosive influences that have had a cancerous effect on the Mafia.

Donnie Brasco

Joseph D. Pistone, alias Donnie Brasco

Two of the men involved in the murder of the three rogue capos were Benjamin "Lefty Guns" Ruggiero and his capo Dominick "Sonny Black" Napolitano. Ruggiero had an associate, Donnie Brasco, whom he proposed for full family membership. In reality, Brasco was undercover FBI agent Joe Pistone, conducting what would become a six-year infiltration of the family.

Pistone's undercover work led to numerous charges against the Bonanno family. Both Ruggiero and Rastelli received lengthy sentences. On August 17, 1981, Napolitano was shot and killed in a basement by Ronald Filocomo and Frank "Curly" Lino as punishment for admitting Pistone to his crew. Anthony Mirra, the man who had brought Pistone to the family, was also killed.

Anthony Mirra

Pistone was on the verge of becoming made when the FBI ordered him to end his operation on July 26, 1981. Pistone wanted to become made, believing that if it got out that a Mafia family had allowed an FBI agent into its ranks, it would destroy its reputation for invincibility. However, Pistone's superiors felt it was too dangerous. After the Donnie Brasco affair, the Mafia Commission removed the Bonanno family from the panel. However, when the federal government pressed charges against the New York Cosa Nostra leadership in the Mafia Commission Trial, the Bonannos avoided indictment. They were thus the only family whose leadership wasn't decimated as a result of the trial. The leaders of the other major families were all sent to prison for life, with the Lucchese family losing its entire hierarchy. As a result, the Bonanno family was able to keep its leadership intact and build up its power again.

Under Massino's command

Rastelli's death in 1991, following a period in which he ruled the family from inside prison, saw the promotion of Massino to the top spot. However, Massino had been the real power in the family since the mid-1980's. One of his first acts was to change the family's name to "the Massino family." Like other Mafiosi, Massino had been very displeased at Bonanno's tell-all book, *A Man of Honor*, and believed he'd broken the code of omertà by writing it. However, the change never stuck, and most people outside the family continued to use the old name.

Remembering the pitfalls that landed other bosses in prison, Massino adopted a more secretive way of doing business. He shut down the family's social clubs, believing they were too easy to bug. He also streamlined the family's chain of command, assigning a group of capos to oversee a particular enterprise and report to underboss Salvatore Vitale. He also barred family members from speaking his name. Instead, they were to point to their ears when referring to him—a nod to how Genovese boss Vincent Gigante told his men to point to their chins rather than use his name. Remembering how close Pistone/Brasco had come to actually becoming made, Massino required any prospective soldier to be "on record" with a made man for at least eight years before becoming made himself. He also strongly encouraged his men to volunteer their sons for membership, believing that they would be less likely to turn informer and be more loyal. However, the family already had a reputation for loyalty; it was the only family that had never seen one of its members turn informer in the seven decades since the Castellammarese War.

Massino not only concentrated on the narcotics trade as had become mandatory for a mob boss, but also in other areas less likely to draw the attention of the authorities than drugs, such as the Mafia's stock trades of racketeering, money laundering and loan sharking. A close friend of Massino's, and boss of the Gambino crime family, John Gotti, also helped to get the Bonannos a seat on the Commission again. Over the next 10 years, the family steadily increased its power. By the mid-1990s, the FBI reckoned Massino as the most powerful Mafia boss in New York and the country. He was the only full-fledged New York boss who wasn't in prison.

Massino turns informant

1970's surveillance picture of Joe Massino

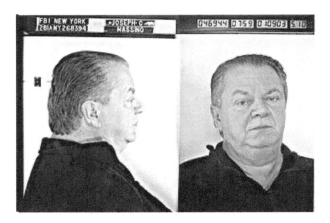

FBI mugshot of Joseph Massino

The family managed to keep its nose clean until 2000, when a pair of forensic accountants who normally worked on financial fraud cases discovered that Barry Weinberg, a businessman who had partnered with capo Richard "Shellackhead" Cantarella in several parking lots, had failed to report millions of dollars' worth of income over a decade. Told he faced a long prison term unless he wore a wire and incriminated his Bonanno partners, Weinberg agreed to cooperate. One of Weinberg's other partners, Augustino Scozzari, also agreed to cooperate. Between them, Weinberg and Scozzari captured hundreds of incriminating statements from Cantrella and his crew.

In October 2002, armed with this evidence, the government won a 24-count RICO indictment against 21 Bonanno soldiers and associates. The biggest names on the indictment were Cantarella—who was serving as acting underboss while Vitale was awaiting sentencing for loansharking and money laundering—and capo Frank Coppa. Within a month of his indictment, Coppa agreed to become a government witness, becoming the first made man in the Bonanno family's history to break his blood oath. Soon after agreeing to cooperate, Coppa directly implicated Massino in the Napolitano murder, and also implicated Cantarella and Vitale in the 1992 murder of *New York Post* delivery superintendent Robert Perrino, who was a Bonanno soldier. Seeing the handwriting on the wall, Cantarella negotiated his own plea bargain in December, and agreed to testify against Massino and Vitale.

Massino and Vitale were charged with the crime in 2003 after two of their capos turned themselves over as witnesses for the government. Vitale also faced charges for the murder of Perrino. Up to this point he had been utterly loyal to his boss. However, Cantarella and Coppa told FBI agents that Massino suspected Vitale was an informer and wanted him killed. When the FBI notified Vitale of this, Vitale decided to switch sides himself. He was followed in rapid succession by four other soldiers and associates. Massino now faced eleven RICO counts, including seven murders. In a separate indictment, Massino was charged with an eighth murder, that of Montreal-based capo Gerlando "George from Canada" Sciascia, which carried the death penalty. With seven of his former henchmen testifying against him, his conviction in July 2004 was a foregone conclusion. Four months later, Massino became the full-time boss of an American crime family to turn informant, sparing himself the ultimate penalty for the murder of Sciascia. By this time, 90 of the family's 150 made men were under indictment.

Massino is believed to be the man who pointed the FBI towards a spot in Ozone Park, Queens, called "The Hole", where the body of Alphonse Indelicato had been found in 1981. Told to dig a little deeper, authorities duly uncovered the remains of Dominick Trinchera and Philip Giaccone, as well as a body suspected to be that of John Favara, a neighbor of Gambino family boss John Gotti who had killed the mobster's son in a car/bicycle accident, and paid with his life.

Massino is also believed to have provided the police with information on a number of high ranking Bonanno Family members and former acting boss Vincent Basciano, whose conversations with Massino were taped in late 2004 and early 2005 by the turncoat himself. Before Massino became an informant himself, his acting boss on the outside was Anthony "Tony Green" Urso, but his tenure was short-lived as he too was imprisoned on numerous charges, leading to Basciano taking control. Vincent Basciano's term as acting boss was hampered with his arrest in late 2004, but with Massino's eventual betrayal, authorities claim that Basciano assumed the top position in 2005, is allegedly the current

Boss and leading the broken Bonanno family from his prison cell.

The authorities continue to plague the family, with the February 16, 2006 arrest of acting boss Michael Mancuso on murder charges, while alleged Boss Vincent Basciano was convicted on charges of conspiracy to murder, attempted murder, and illegal gambling and was sentenced to life imprisonment in late 2007. The main charge against him was that he conspired to murder both the judge and prosecutor in the case, as well as Patrick DeFilippo, a fellow Bonanno crime family captain.

Basciano's leadership

Vincent Basciano

Bonanno family Boss Vincent Basciano named Brooklyn
business owner Salvatore "Sal the Ironworker" Montagna,
as the new "acting boss" of the Bonanno Family.
Sometimes referred to as "Sal the Zip" due to his Sicilian
birth, Montagna was closely associated with the Bonanno
Sicilian faction, including Baldo Amato and capo Cesare
Bonventre. Montagna started as a soldier in capo Patrick
"Patty from the Bronx" DeFilippo's crew. In 2003,
Montagna became *acting capo* after DeFilippo's arrest on
murder and racketeering charges. Law enforcement sources
have stated that Salvatore Montagna was tabbed as "acting
boss" with Vincent Basciano's consent to maintain the
Bonanno Family's base of power within the Bronx faction
of the Bonanno crime family.

The Bonanno family's base of power was traditionally held
by the Brooklyn faction from the time of Family patriarch
Joseph Bonanno until the eventual rise of Queens faction

leader Philip "Rusty" Rastelli in the early 1970's. The ascension of the Bronx faction began with Basciano's promotion to acting boss, eventual ascension to the top position of Boss, continued through Michael Mancuso's short tenure and now remains with Sal Montagna acting on behalf of Basciano.

In July 2004, *The New York Times* reported that federal prosecutors in Brooklyn "say that overall, in the last four years, they have won convictions against roughly 75 mobsters or associates in a crime clan with fewer than 150 made members." In February 2005, Bonanno family Capo Anthony "Tony Green" Urso pleaded guilty to racketeering, murder, gambling, loan sharking and extortion charges, while Capo Joseph "Joe Saunders" Cammarano, along with soldier Louis Restivo pleaded guilty to murder and racketeering charges."

Twelve Bonanno family member and associates, seven over the age 70, including acting consigliere Anthony "Mr. Fish" Rabito and respected soldier Salvatore Scudiero were indicted and arrested on June 14, 2005 on charges of operating a $10 million a year gambling ring."

The defection of former Bonanno family Bosses Joseph Massino and Salvatore Vitale, along with four high ranking former Capos, has caused the Bonanno family to lose power, influence and respect within the New York underworld to a degree not seen since the Donnie Brasco incident. With Nicholas "Nicky Mouth" Santora as "acting underboss" for the imprisoned Michael Mancuso, and Anthony Rabito as the alleged *consigliere*, Montagna was capable of running the day-to-day operations on behalf of Vincent Basciano. On February 6, 2007 acting underboss Nicholas Santora, acting consigliere Anthony Rabito, captains or former captains Jerome Asaro, Joseph

Cammarano, Jr. and Louis Decicco were indicted on racketeering charges.

The Last Don

Joseph Massino

Joseph Massino, the man who organized the hits on the three rebel capos, succeeded Rusty Rastelli as boss of the Bonanno Family, not an enviable job with the family in such disarray and still banished from the Commission. But Massino proved to be remarkably adept at turning things around. According to journalist Jerry Capeci, Massino surrounded himself with loyalists, shut down the Bonanno social clubs, and tried to adopt a more secretive manner of doing business. To foil wiretaps, he insisted that his name never be mentioned. Instead, members were to point to their ears when referring to him. His efforts succeeded, and the Bonanno Family was able to reestablish itself in the traditional mob rackets while reorganizing its profitable drug operations. The rejuvenated family was able to regain its seat on the Commission, and while the bosses of the other four New York families faced indictments and convictions in the 1990s, Massino managed to elude prosecutors, earning him the title, the Last Don.

The family prospered under Massino, and unlike the other New York families, the Bonannos did not suffer from turncoats within their ranks. But then in 2003 Massino and his brother-in-law Salvatore Vitale were charged with RICO violations and murder in the rubout of Sonny Black Napolitano. Vitale, who was facing another murder charge separately, decided to turn states witness against Massino to help himself.

Salvatore Vitale

Vitale proved to be a very informative stool pigeon for the feds, singing songs of murder and mayhem that rivaled even Gambino-family turncoat Sammy Bull Gravano's testimonies in the early 1990s. Vitale directed the FBI to a known Mafia burial ground in Ozone Park, Queens, which had been used in the late 1970s and early 80s.

This was the marshy lot where the body of Sonny Red Indelicato had been found in the weeks after his murder in May 1981.

Sammy "Bull" Gravano in court

In October 2004 the feds returned to the site and dug deeper. In the mud they found the skeletal remains of three bodies, a credit card with Dominick Trinchera's name on it, and a Piaget wristwatch similar to one that Lucky Philly Giaccone had been wearing the day he disappeared. Investigators suspected that the third body was the remains of John Favara, a furniture store manager and neighbor of the late Gambino boss John Gotti. Favara had disappeared in 1980 after he accidentally ran over Gottis 12-year-old son Frank, killing the boy. Mob informants told authorities that the three rebel Bonanno capos had been buried by Gambino soldiers as a favor from Mr. Gotti to Mr. Massino, according to the *New York Times*.

In July 2004 a jury found Joseph Massino guilty of orchestrating a quarter-century of murder, racketeering, arson, extortion, loan-sharking, and gambling, the Associated Press reported, running the family from his Queens restaurant, Casablanca.

Gerlando Sciascia

On the heels of this conviction, federal prosecutors filed new charges against Massino in the murder of Gerlando George from Canada Sciascia who had moved to New York in 1997 after being deported from Canada for being a public menace. As reported on *Ganglandnews.com,* Massino had ordered Sciascia's murder when Sciascia had the temerity to accuse one of Massino's favorite capos of being a coke fiend. U.S. Attorney General John Ashcroft, a few days before announcing his resignation from office in November 2004 - and perhaps acting a bit like a don himself - ordered prosecutors to seek the death penalty against Massino in this trial. If convicted, Massino could become the first Mafia member to face execution since the federal death penalty was reinstated in 1988.

The last organized-crime figure to be executed in the United States was Louis Lepke Buchalter who was given the electric chair in 1944.

Rastelli took over once again, but the family's internal strife was far from over. Three renegade capos - Philip Giaccone, Alphonse "Sonny Red" Indelicato and Dominick "Big Trin" Trinchera - began to openly question Rastelli's leadership and apparently to plot to overthrow him. With the blessing of the other families, Rastelli had the three men wiped out in a hit arranged by then-street boss Dominick "Sonny Black" Napolitano, as well as the future Boss Joseph "Big Joe" Massino.

In August 2006, the alleged boss of the Montreal Cosa Nostra, Vito Rizzuto, was extradited from Canada to the United States to face charges in the 1981 murder in New York of the three Bonanno captains. Vito Rizzuto was released from prison in Colorado and returned to Toronto, Canada, on October 5, 2012.

Current position of

The Family

Under the rule of former Boss Joseph Massino, the Bonanno family climbed back to the top of New York's crime family hierarchy and once again became a top power in America's underworld, but high level defections and convictions have left the family a shell of its former self once more during its long criminal history. Vincent Basciano is serving a prison sentence for racketeering and Salvatore Montagna has been deported to Canada. Both were appointed acting bosses during Massino's imprisonment and after Massino's defection to the FBI.

A March 2009 article in the New York Post stated that Salvatore Montagna was the acting boss of the Bonanno crime family. The article also stated that the Bonanno family current consists of approximately 115 "made" members. Montagna was later deported to Canada in April 2009 leaving the family to create a ruling panel until a new boss was chosen.

On January 11, 2010 Jerry Capeci quoted sources as saying that Nicholas Santora and Anthony Rabito, who were both released from prison in 2009 and are still unable to meet freely with their fellow wiseguys, are supporting capo Vincent Asaro to become the new boss of the family. Asaro also has close ties to Queens-based mobsters from the Lucchese, Gambino and Genovese families who have voiced their support for him, sources say. A key player in the recent talks is Vito Grimaldi, who is viewed as an adviser to the Zips (Sicilian mobsters in the United States). Capeci's sources say Asaro, who for many years has had dealings as both a mob supervisor and cohort of Sicilian wiseguys, may win Grimaldi's support. Another candidate with key Sicilian backing is current acting boss Vincent Badalamenti. Due to Joseph Massino deciding to cooperate with the FBI, both sides agree that the family will no longer take orders from the man he previously appointed acting boss, Vincent Basciano.

In January 2012, prosecutors indicted the hierarchy of the Bonanno family on racketeering and extortion charges. These charges were primarily based on information from government informant Hector Pagan. Those arrested were Nicholas Santora, James LaForte, Vincent Badalamenti, and soldiers Vito Balsamo and Anthony Calabrese. All five defendants pleaded guilty to lesser charges and were given sentences ranging from six to 18 months. Anthony Graziano (Pagan's ex father-in-law), who was arrested in 2011, was sentenced to one and a half years in prison.

In June 2013, Michael Mancuso, who is currently imprisoned was named the new official boss of the family. Mancuso is first man to hold this title since boss Joseph Massino became a government witness in 2005. Mancuso controls all decision making from prison while his underboss Thomas DiFiore is running the family on the streets.

Historical leadership

Boss (official and acting)

ca. 1908–1911 — Salvatore Bonanno — returned to Sicily

1911–1921 — Vito Bonventre — stepped down

1921–1930 — Nicola Schirò — fled

1930–1931 — Salvatore Maranzano — murdered on September 10, 1931

1931–1968 — Giuseppe "Joseph" Bonanno — replaced by the Commission

1965–1966 — Gaspar "Gasparino" DiGregorio — installed and replaced by the Commission

1966–1971 — Paul Sciacca — imprisoned

1971–1973 — Natale "Joe Diamonds" Evola — died on August 23, 1973

1973–1991 — Phillip "Rusty" Rastelli — imprisoned 1975–1984 and 1986–1991

Acting 1974–1979 — Carmine "Cigar" Galante — murdered on July 12, 1979

Acting 1979–1983 — Salvatore "Sally Fruits" Farrugia — appointed by the Commission

Acting 1987–1991 — Anthony "Old Man" Spero

1991–2004 — Joseph "Big Joe" Massino — imprisoned January 2003, became government informant in October 2004

Acting 1991–1993 — Anthony "Old Man" Spero

Acting 2003–2004 — Anthony "Tony Green" Urso — imprisoned January 2004

"Acting" 2004–2009 — Vincent "Vinny Gorgeous" Basciano — imprisoned November 2004, in July 2007 receiving a life sentence

Acting 2004–2006 — Michael "the Nose" Mancuso — imprisoned February 2006

Acting 2006–2009 — Salvatore "Sal the Iron Worker" Montagna — deported to Canada in April 2009

"Acting" 2010–2012 — Vincent "Vinny TV." Badalamenti — imprisoned in January 2012

2013–present — Michael "the Nose" Mancuso

Acting 2013–present — Thomas "Tommy D" DiFiore

Street Boss

The *Street Boss* is responsible for passing on orders to lower ranking members. In some instances a *Ruling panel* (of capos) substituted the Street boss role. The family may choose to assemble a ruling panel of capos if the boss dies, goes to prison, or is incapacitated. During the 1960s family war, a ruling panel of capos controlled the decision making of the family.

1964–1968 — Frank Labruzzo — led Bonanno faction

1964– *Ruling panel* — Gasparino DiGregorio, Angelo Caruso, Nicolino Alfano, Joseph Notaro, Thomas D'Angelo, Natale Evola, Joseph DeFilippo, Peter Crociata and Paul Sciacca

1964–1965 — *Ruling panel* — Gasparino DiGregorio, Angelo Caruso, and Nicolino Alfano

1979–1981 — Salvatore "Toto" Catalano — leader of the Sicilian faction, became Underboss

1981— Dominick "Sonny Black" Napolitano — murdered on August 17, 1981

2009–2010 — *Ruling panel* — Joseph Sammartino, Sr. (capo in New Jersey), the other members are unknown

2012–2013 — *Ruling panel* — Vincent Asaro, Anthony Rabito, and Thomas DiFiore

Underboss
(Official and acting)

1915–1921 — Stefano Magaddino — fled to Buffalo

1921–1930 — Vito Bonventre — murdered on July 15, 1930

1930–1932 — Angelo Caruso

1932–1955 — Francesco "Frank Caroll" Garofalo

1955–1957 — Carmine "Lilo" Galante — indicted and fled

1957–1968 — John "Johnny Burns" Morales

Acting 1965–1968 — Pietro "Skinny Pete" Crociata — for the *DiGregorio faction*

Acting 1968 — Frank "Russo" Mari — for the *DiGregorio faction*, murdered

1968–1971 — Natale "Joe Diamonds" Evola — became boss

1971–1973 — Phillip "Rusty" Rastelli — became boss

1974–1979 — Nicholas "Nicky Glasses" Marangello (demoted)

1979–1981 — Salvatore "Sal" Catalano (leader of the Sicilian faction)

1981–1988 — Joseph "Big Joe" Massino (imprisoned in 1984)

Acting 1984–1988 — Louis "Louie Ha Ha" Attanasio

1991–2004 — Salvatore "Handsome Sal" Vitale (became FBI informant in October 2004)

Acting 2001–2003 — Richard "Shellackhead" Cantarella (became an FBI informant on December 2002, and in June 2004 testified against Bonanno boss Joseph Massino.)

Acting 2003–2004 — Joseph "Joe C." Cammarano, Sr.

Acting 2004 — Michael "the Nose" Mancuso — became acting boss

Acting 2004–2007 — Nicholas "Nicky Mouth" Santora (indicted in 2007)

2013–present — Thomas Defiore

Consigliere

(Official and acting)

c.1930s - Frank Italiano

1932–1939 — Phillipe Rapa

1940–1964 — John Tartamella

1964–1968 — Salvatore "Bill" Bonanno

Acting 1965–1968 — Nicolino "Nick" Alfano — for the *DiGregorio faction*

Acting 1968 — Michael "Mike" Adamo

1968–1971 — Phillip "Rusty" Rastelli (Promoted to underboss in 1971)

1971–1974 — Joseph DiFilippo

1974–1984 — Stefano "Stevie Beefs" Cannone

1984–2001 — Anthony Spero (acting boss from 1987–1993, died September 29, 2008)

Acting 1987–1992 — Joseph Buccellato

Acting 1999–2001 — Anthony "T.G." Graziano

2001–2010 — Anthony "T.G." Graziano

Acting 2001–2003 — Anthony "Tony Green" Urso — became acting boss

Acting 2004–2007 — Anthony "Fat Tony" Rabito — imprisoned

Current family members

Administration

Boss Michael "the Nose" Mancuso — is currently incarcerated with a projected release date from prison of March 12, 2019.

Underboss Thomas "Tommy D" DiFiore

Consigliere Unknown

Capos

Brooklyn faction

Vincent "Vinny TV." Badalamenti — the former acting boss. In December 2009, Badalamenti was found with Staten Island-based capo Anthony Calabrese and soldier John "Johnny Green" Faracithe meeting at a Bensonhurst storefront. He served as acting boss from early 2010 until 2012 when he was imprisoned.

(*In prison*) Nicholas "Nicky Mouth" Santora — capo controlling the *Motion Lounge crew* active in the *Western Brooklyn* communities of Williamsburg and East Williamsburg among others. Santora took over as *acting underboss* in 2004, when Joseph Massino and Salvatore Vitale became government witnesses. In 2007, Santora was indicted on racketeering and extortion charges. He is currently imprisoned with a projected release date of October 23, 2013.

(*In prison*) Anthony "T.G." Graziano — capo operating in Brooklyn and Staten Island. Graziano is the former consigliere of the family. He operated a pension fund scheme that eventually reaped over $11.7 million from elderly investors and supervised a large narcotics trafficking operation in Florida. In 2002, Graziano was imprisoned on federal racketeering and murder charges. In January 2012, Graziano was indicted on new racketeering charges. He is in custody pending trial.

Joseph Cammarano, Sr. — capo operating a crew in Brooklyn with his son Joseph "Joe Saunders" Cammarano, Jr. His son Joe, Jr. has been in the Bonanno family since 1990s under Joseph Massino. In 2007, Joe, Jr. was indicted for racketeering, conspiracy, illegal gambling, extortion, loansharking and drug trafficking.

Anthony "Anthony from Elmont" Mannone — (aka *Anthony from the Five Towns*) — capo who was arrested on February 24, 2010 for running an illegal gambling and extortion ring throughout Brooklyn. Mannone was released from prison on June 27, 2013

Louis "Louie Electric" DeCicco — capo in Brooklyn with operations in Queens and Long Island. In March 2007, DeCicco was arrested along with other Bonanno capos. On December 31, 2009, DeCicco was released from prison.

Staten Island faction

Anthony Calabrese — capo based in Staten Island. He was found with capo Vincent Badalamenti on December 2009 meeting at a Bensonhurst storefront for a Christmas party.

Anthony Furino — capo based in Staten Island. In 2004, Furino was arrested for extortion of Long Island night clubs and Staten Island restaurants. In 2007, Furino was released from prison.

(*In prison*) Anthony "Scal" Sclafani — capo in the Staten Island faction who operates illegal gambling. Sclafani also operates in New Jersey with capo Joseph Sammartino, Sr. On October 14, 2009, Sclafani was arrested on loansharking charges. Sclafani is currently imprisoned. His projected release date is February 14, 2014.

Frank Porco — 70 year-old capo operating from Staten Island, Brooklyn and Florida. In 2005, Calabrese was released from prison.

(*In prison*) Gerard "Jerry" Chilli — capo in the Staten Island faction. Chilli along with his nephew Tom Fiore controlled operations in Broward County, Florida and Hollywood, Florida.

Manhattan faction

Joseph Indelicato — capo in Manhattan and New Jersey. Took over crew of from his deceased brother, Alphonse "Sonny Red" Indelicato. Joseph's nephew Anthony "Bruno" Indelicato is a soldier in the crew.

William "Willie Glasses" Riviello — capo operating in Manhattan, Brooklyn, Queens, Bronx and Westchester County. In 2004, Riviello was arrested for a stolen bank check scheme in the Bronx and Yonkers, New York, that grossed over $500,000 for the family. In 2007, Riviello was released from prison.

Queens faction

Vincent "Vinny" Asaro — capo since the 1980's. During the 1990s, Asaro allegedly operated a multi-million-dollar stolen car ring and oversaw the hijacking of cargo at John F. Kennedy International Airport. In 1995, Asaro was convicted of racketeering and enterprise corruption and sentenced to more than five years in prison.

Anthony "Fat Tony" Rabito — capo. Rabito was the former acting Consigliere for Vincent Basciano prior to his incarceration and a longtime member of the Bonanno family. From January 2003 to July 2004, Rabito operated an illegal gambling and loansharking ring in Brooklyn, Queens, Manhattan, and Staten Island, earning $210,000 a week. Currently on trial for RICO charges.

Bronx faction

(*In prison*) Patrick "Patty From the Bronx" DeFilippo —
capo operating in the Bronx and ally to the Sicilian faction.
DeFilippo was incarcerated on racketeering charges and
acting boss Salvatore Montagna took his crew. DeFilippo's
projected released date is June 25, 2038.

New Jersey faction

Joseph "Sammy" Sammartino, Sr. — capo in the New
Jersey faction since 2003. Sammartino lives in North
Arlington, New Jersey and is part of the current ruling
panel/committee. His crew is based in Bayonne, New
Jersey. On October 14, 2009, Sammartino was arrested on
loansharking charges He was sentenced to 18 months in
prison and a $50,000 dollar fine for extortion. On January
27, 2011, Sammartino was released from prison.

Soldiers

Sandro Aiosa - a former capo in the 1970s who operated in Brooklyn. Aiosa is currently in federal prison. His projected release date is October 12, 2012.

Joseph "Joe Lefty" Loiacono - former acting capo who was arrested on October 14, 2009 for running a loansharking operation. Currently in prison, his projected release date is May 18, 2012.

Anthony "Little Anthony" Pipitone - former acting capo arrested on October 14, 2009. Pipitone is currently incarcerated in federal prison. His project release date is February 7, 2013.

Jerome Asaro - a former acting capo with large illegal gambling and loansharking rings in Queens. Asaro is the son of Vincent Asaro. In February 2007, Jerome Asaro pleaded guilty to a 25-year association with the Bonanno family. On November 2, 2010, Asaro was released from prison. **Joseph "Joe Saunders, Jr." Cammarano, Jr.** - his father Joseph Cammarano, Sr. is a Bonanno family capo. Joseph, Jr., served in the U.S. Navy for six years before joining the Bonanno crime family. In February 2007, he was arrested on racketeering charges. In January 2009, Joseph, Jr. was released from federal prison.

Salvatore "Toto" Catalano - a former capo and Street boss of the Sicilian faction. Catalano was heavily involved in the Pizza Connection a heroin drug distribution scheme with boss Carmine Galante. The heroin was shipped into the U.S. and sold through pizzerias in New York City and New Jersey. In 1976, Catalano became capo of the *Knickerbocker Avenue Crew*. On March 2, 1987, Catalano was sentenced to 45 years in prison and fined $1.15 million. He was released from prison on November 16, 2009.

(In prison) **Joseph "Joe Desi" DeSimone** - a former capo. DeSimone was involved in the 1981 murders of Philip Giaccone, Dominick Trinchera and Alphonse Indelicato.

Imprisoned soldiers

Baldassare "Baldo" Amato - a soldier in the Sicilian faction and leader of a freelance crew operating in Ridgewood, Queens. Amato is serving a life sentence in federal prison.

Louis "Louie Ha Ha" Attanasio - a former capo in the Bronx. Attanasio along with his brother Robert and Peter Calabrese murdered Bonanno family Sicilian faction member Cesare Bonventre in 1984. On September 20, 2006 Attanasio and Peter Calabrese were sentenced to 15 years in prison for the 1984 Bonventre murder. Attanasio's projected release date is January 23, 2018.

Peter "Peter Rabbit" Calabrese - a former capo involved in the 1984 murder of Cesare Bonventre with brothers Louis and Robert Attanasio. In 2006, Calabrese and Louis Attanasio were sentenced to 15 years for Cesare Bonventre's murder. Calabrese's projected release date is February 13, 2017.

Thomas Fiore - former "acting capo" of Gerard Chilli's South Florida crew. He is based in Palm Beach County, city of Boynton Beach. On October 14, 2009 his crew in South Florida was charged under the RICO law. Six of the eleven crew members pleaded guilty to a list of crimes. The members that plead guilty included crew enforcer Pasquale

Rubbo his brother Joseph Rubbo. The crew is involved in arson, insurance fraud, identity theft, illegal gambling and other crimes. They send some tribute up to Bonanno family bosses in New York City. On March 2, 2010 Fiore was sentenced to twelve years for racketeering. His projected release date is January 18, 2020.

Anthony "Bruno" Indelicato - soldier in the crew of his uncle, Joseph Indelicato and the son of Alphonse "Sonny Red" Indelicato. A *made member* since the late 1970s, Anthony Indelicato may have participated in the 1979 murder of Carmine Galante. Indelicato was a defendant in 1986 Mafia Commission Trial he was sentenced to 45 years and was released in 2000. On December 16, 2008 Indelicato received a 20 year prison sentence for the 2001 killing of Frank Santoro. Indelicato's projected release date is May 20, 2023.

Thomas Pitera - soldier and hitman who was sentenced to life in federal prison. He is currently serving his sentence in federal prison.

Anthony "Tony Green" Urso - former capo and acting capo under Joseph Massino in the 1990s. In 2004, Urso was imprisoned for extortion and loansharking. Currently in prison, his projected release date is December 5, 2021.

Former members

Cesare "The Tall Guy" Bonventre - a former capo and member of the Sicilian faction. He was related to Vito Bonventre, John Bonventre, and Joseph Bonanno. He was murdered on April 16, 1984.

John "Boobie" Cerasani – was a Bonanno family soldier and right-hand man to Sonny "Black" Napolitano. Cerasani was involved in the 1981 murders of three warring captains Alphonse Indelicato, Dominick Trinchera and Philip Giaccone. In July 26, 1982 Cerasani, Benjamin "Lefty" Ruggiero, Anthony Rabito, Nicholas Santora and Antonio Tomasulo were tried at a Manhattan federal district court. Cerasani was later acquitted.

James "Jimmy Legs" Episcopia - a soldier who worked for capo Sonny "Black" Napolitano.

Salvatore "Sal the Iron Worker" Montagna - Capo and acting boss after the 2005 conviction of Vincent Basciano. Based in the Bronx, Montagna was reportedly the leader of the Sicilian faction. Montagna was born in Montreal, Canada and resided in Elmont, New York. His family originated from Castellammare del Golfo, Sicily. On April 21, 2009, Montagna was deported to Canada. The Rizzuto crime family led by Vito Rizzuto allowed Montagna to work with his family but would not take orders from him. Montagna was assassinated on November 24, 2011, outside of Montreal, his body was found near Repentigny, Quebec, in the Assomption River, on Île Vaudry, having been shot at around 10 am.

Gerlando "George from Canada" Sciascia - a former capo who operated out of Montreal, Canada and worked with the

Sicilian faction in New York. Sciascia served as mediator between Bonanno family and Montreal's Rizzuto family in the early 1990s. He was murdered on March 18, 1999.

Michael Zaffarano – a former capo who was involved in the adult entertainment industry. Anthony Mirra a soldier in his crew was responsible for allowing FBI agent Joseph D. Pistone ("Donnie Brasco") to work undercover in the Bonanno crime family. On February 14, 1980, Zaffarano died from a heart attack during an FBI raid.

Family crews

The Sicilian faction - in the 1950s the Bonanno family started bringing Sicilian-born Mafia members to New York to keep closer ties with the Sicilian Mafia families. American mobsters frequently refer to these Sicilian mobsters as Zips. The derogatory term name derives from their Sicilian birth and their fast-spoken, difficult-to-understand Sicilian dialects.

The Motion Lounge crew - run by underboss and capo Nicholas "Nicky Mouth" Santora. This Brooklyn-based crew is active primarily in the Western Brooklyn communities of Williamsburg and East Williamsburg.

The Indelicato crew - run by capo Joseph Indelicato. This crew is active in Manhattan and New Jersey. Indelicato's nephew Anthony "Bruno" Indelicato is a soldier in this crew.

Bath Beach crew - was run by consigliere Anthony Spero until his death in 2008.

Phoenix crew - possibly inactive after retiring of Joe Bonanno.

Allied

Criminal organization

The Bonannos and the Canadian faction - In the mid-1950s, Carmine Galante established two groups to control the illegal rackets in Montreal, Canada. The *Sicilian group* was led by Luigi Greco and the *Calabrian group* was led by Vic Cotroni. The Montreal groups became part of the Bonanno crime family having made members in each group. Joseph Bonanno promoted Vic Controni to become the boss (capo) of both Montreal groups. In 1964, Sicilian group leader Pasquale Cuntrera was arrested and Nicolo "Nick" Rizzuto took over the group starting a war in 1973. The Sicilians killed the Cotroni-Calabrian group underboss Paolo Violi and others. With the death of Vic Controni in 1984, the Rizzuto crime family became the most powerful Mafia family in Montreal, Canada. In 1988, Nick Rizzuto was convicted of cocaine trafficking and his son Vittorio "Vito" Rizzuto became boss of the family. By 1999 the Rizzuto crime family began working independently, while remaining allies to the Bonanno family. Vito Rizzuto was arrested in January 2004 and extradited to the United States on murder charges in August 2006. In May 2007, Rizzuto accepted a plea deal for his involvement in the May 1981 murders of three renegade Bonanno capos in New York. He was sentenced to ten years in prison, with a projected release date of October 2012. However, after his release, Rizzuto faces the possibility of extradition to Italy to face conspiracy and money laundering charges concerning the Straits of Messina Bridge project there. On November 10, 2010, Nick Rizzuto was killed at his residence in the Cartierville borough of Montreal.

Government informants and witnesses

Joseph "Big Joe" Massino – former boss from early 1990s until 2004. Massino became the first official boss from New York to become an informant. While boss, Massino changed the Bonanno family from being the weakest family in New York City to one of the most powerful in the country. He teamed up with Gambino family boss John Gotti to reinstate the Bonanno family on the Mafia Commission. In the early 2000s, Massino was the strongest and most influential boss not in prison. In January 2003, Massino was charged with the 1981 murder of Bonanno capo Dominick Napolitano. Massino had Napolitano killed for admitting FBI agent Joseph D. Pistone (known as Donnie Brasco) to his crew. In 2004, Massino turned informant and testified against members of his own family to avoid the death penalty. In January 2005, Massino wore a surveillance device to record conversations in prison with his acting boss Vincent Basciano.

Salvatore "Handsome Sal" Vitale – former underboss. In January 2003, Vitale was charged with the 1992 murder of Bonanno associate Robert Perrino. in April 2003, Vitale became a government informant. In July 2004, he testified at the trial of his brother-in-law, boss Joseph Massino. As of 2010, Vitale has testified against 51 organized crime figures.

Richard Cantarella – former underboss. In December 2002, Cantarella became one of the first Bonanno government witnesses. In January 2003, Cantarella was indicted for the 1991 murder of Bonanno associate Robert Perrino. In June 2004, Cantarella testified against boss Joseph Massino.

Cantarella's wife Lauretta, his son Paul, a Bonanno soldier, and cousin Joseph D'Amico, a Bonanno capo, also became government witnesses.

Frank Coppa, Sr. - former capo. Became a government witness in November 2002.

Frank "Curly" Lino – former capo. Became the first government witness in Bonanno history. Lino testified at the trial for the 1981 murders of Bonanno capos Alphonse Indelicato, Philip Giaccone, and Dominick Trinchera. Lino then testified on the 1981 murder of Dominick Napolitano. Napolitano was killed by Bonanno family member Robert Lino, Sr. (his cousin) and Ronald Filocomo.

James "Big Louie" Tartaglione – former capo. In 2003, Tartaglione began wearing a surveillance device and recorded conversations with other Bonanno family members. In 2007, Tartaglione testified against Vincent Basciano and Patrick DeFilippo.

Paul "Paulie" Cantarella - former soldier and son of Bonanno capo Richard Cantarella. In 2002, Paul became government witness with his father and his mother Lauretta.

Joseph "Joey Moak" D'Amico – former soldier in the crew of his uncle, Bonanno capo Alfred "Al Walker" Embarrato's. D'Amico was arrested for the murder of his cousin Anthony Mirra, who had allowed FBI agent Joseph Pistone to work for the family. In March 2003, D'Amico decided to become a government informant.

Dominick Cicale – former capo and former friend of acting capo Vincent Basciano. In 2007, Cicale became a government witness and testified against Basciano.

Nicholas "P.J" Pisciotti – former acting capo. In 2007, Pisciotti assaulted several Genovese crime family associates in a Little Italy restaurant. When Pisciotti learned that Bonanno mobsters Nicholas Santora and Anthony Rabito had given the Genovese family permission to kill him, Pisciotti became a government witness. In 2007, he testified against Vincent Basciano.

Joseph Calco – former associate with the *Bath Avenue crew*. In 2001, Calco became a government witness and testified against Bonanno Consigliere Anthony Spero. Calco then entered the Witness Protection Program under the name "Joseph Milano". While working in Florida, Calco got into a fight and his true identity became public knowledge.

Michael "Mikey Y" Yammine – former associate with the *Bath Avenue crew*. In 2001, Yammine became a government informant and testified against Bonanno consigliere Anthony Spero.

Duane "Goldie" Leisenheimer – a family associate and ally to Joseph Massino since the age of twelve. He joined the Massino hijacking crew and helped hide Massino in 1980s. Leisenheimer was the lookout for the 1981 murder of three captains. In 2004 with Salvatore Vital testifying against him, Leisenheimer turned informant against Massino. Chris "King of South Beach" Paciello - former associate of the Bonanno and Colombo crime families. In 1993, Paciello became a government informant.

Hearings

In popular culture

The 1997 film *Donnie Brasco* tells the story of how FBI agent Joseph D. Pistone was able to work undercover with the Bonanno crime family and almost became a made man. The film was directed by Mike Newell, Written by Joseph D. Pistone and starred Al Pacino and Johnny Depp.

In the video game GTA 4 the *Messina crime family* is based on the Bonanno crime family. The Messina family is said to return its lost power back in the last years because of their alliance with Jon Gravelli. This is like the Bonanno family 1990s turn around becoming a powerful force on the commission again after John Gotti helped them regain their lost seat. They have a stronghold in Dukes the GTA 4 version of Queens like the real life Bonannos and also are involved in construction business.

The 1999 film *Bonanno: A Godfather's Story* is an autobiography of boss Joseph "Joe Bananas" Bonanno. Directed by Michel Poulette, the film was based on the book written by Bill and Joseph Bonanno. Joseph was played by Martin Landau, Tony Nardi. and Bruce Ramsay.

Colombo Crime Family

The **Colombo crime family** is the youngest of the "Five Families" that dominates organized crime activities in New York City, United States, within the nationwide criminal organization known as the Mafia (or *Cosa Nostra*).

In 1928, Joseph Profaci formed the *Profaci crime family*. Profaci would rule his family without interruption or challenge until the late 1950s. The family has been torn by three internal wars. The first war took place during the late 1950s when capo Joe Gallo revolted against Profaci. The first war lost momentum in the early 1960s when Gallo was arrested and Profaci died of cancer. The family then came together under boss Joseph Colombo. In 1971, the second family war began after Gallo's release from prison and the shooting of Colombo. Colombo supporters led by Carmine Persico won the second war after the exiling of the Gallo crew to the Genovese family in 1975. The family would now enjoy over 15 years of peace under Persico and his string of acting bosses.

In 1991, the third and bloodiest war erupted when acting boss Victor Orena tried to seize power from the imprisoned Carmine Persico. The family split into factions loyal to Orena and Persico and two years of mayhem ensued. In 1993, with 12 family members dead and Orena imprisoned, Persico was the winner more or less by default. He was left with a family decimated by war. In the 2000s, the family was crippled by multiple convictions in federal racketeering cases and numerous members becoming government witnesses. Most observers believe that the Colombo crime family is the weakest of the Five Families of New York City.

Origins

In September 1921, Joseph Profaci arrived in New York City from Villabate, Sicily, Italy. After struggling in Chicago with his businesses, Profaci moved back to Brooklyn in 1925 and become a well-known olive oil importer. On September 27, Profaci obtained his American citizenship. With his olive oil importing business doing well, Profaci made deals with friends from his old town in Sicily and one of his largest buyers was Tampa mobster Ignazio Italiano. Profaci controlled a small criminal gang that operated mainly in Brooklyn. The dominant Cosa Nostra groups in Brooklyn were led by Salvatore D'Aquila, Frankie Yale, Giuseppe Masseria, and Nicola Schirò.

On July 1, 1928, Brooklyn mobster Frankie Yale was murdered by Chicago Outfit boss Al Capone's hit-men. Capone murdered Yale because Yale refused to give Capone, a Neapolitan, control over the Unione Siciliana fraternal association. Yale's murder allowed Profaci and his brother in-law Joseph Magliocco to gain territory for their small gang. Profaci's gang gained territory in Bensonhurst,

Bay Ridge, Red Hook and Carroll Gardens while the rest of Yale's group went to the Masseria family.

On October 10, 1928, the *capo di tutti capi*, Salvatore "Toto" D'Aquila, was murdered, resulting in a fight for D'Aquila's territory. To prevent a gang war in Brooklyn, a Mafia meeting was called on December 5, 1928, at the Statler Hotel in Cleveland, Ohio. The site was chosen because it was neutral territory outside New York under Porrello crime family control and protection. The main topic was dividing D'Aquila's territory. Attendees representing Brooklyn included Profaci, Magliocco, Vincent Mangano (who reported to D'Aqulia family boss Alfred "Al Mineo" Manfredi), Joseph Bonanno (who represented Salvatore Maranzano and the Castellammarese Clan), Chicago mobsters Joseph Guinta and Pasquale Lolordo, and Tampa mobster Ignazio Italiano. At the end of the meeting, Profaci received a share of D'Aquila's Brooklyn territory, with Magliocco as his second-in-command.

The Castellammarese War

The **Castellammarese War** was a bloody power struggle for control of the Italian-American Mafia between partisans of Joe "The Boss" Masseria and those of Salvatore Maranzano. It was so called because Maranzano was based in Castellammare del Golfo, Sicily. Maranzano's faction won, and he declared himself *capo di tutti capi* ("boss of all bosses"), the undisputed leader of the entire Mafia. However, he was soon murdered in turn by a faction of young upstarts led by Lucky Luciano, who established a power-sharing arrangement called "The Commission," a group of five Mafia families of equal stature, to avoid such wars in the future.

Mafia operations in the United States in the 1920s were controlled by Giuseppe "Joe The Boss" Masseria, whose faction consisted mainly of gangsters from Sicily, and the Calabria and Campania regions of Southern Italy. Masseria's faction included Charles "Lucky" Luciano, Albert "Mad Hatter" Anastasia, Vito Genovese, Alfred Mineo, Willie Moretti, Joe Adonis, and Frank Costello.

Powerful Sicilian Mafioso, Don Vito Ferro, decided to make a bid for control of Mafia operations in the United States. From his base in Castellammare del Golfo, he sent Salvatore Maranzano to seize control. The Castellammarese faction in the U.S. included Joseph "Joe Bananas" Bonanno, Stefano "The Undertaker" Magaddino, Joseph Profaci, and Joe Aiello.

Outwardly, the Castellammarese War was between the forces of Masseria and Maranzano. Underneath, however, there was also a generational conflict between the old guard Sicilian leadership, known as the "Mustache Petes" for their long mustaches and old-world ways, and the "Young Turks", a younger and more diverse Italian group who were more forward thinking and willing to work more with non-Italians. Tensions between the Maranzano and Masseria factions were evident as far back as 1928, with one side frequently hijacking the other's alcohol trucks (alcohol production was then illegal in the United States due to Prohibition). However, both factions were fluid, with many mobsters switching sides or killing their own allies during this war.

Months after the D'Aquila murder, Joe Masseria began a campaign to become Capo di tutti capi ('Boss of Bosses') in the United States demanding tribute from the remaining three Mafia groups in New York City which included the Reina family, the Castellammarese Clan and the *Profaci family*. Castellammarese Clan boss Salvatore Maranzano began his own campaign to become 'boss of bosses', this started the Castellammarese War. Masseria along with his ally Alfred Manfredi, the new boss of the D'Aquila family ordered the murder of Gaetano Reina. Masseria believed that Reina was going to support Maranzano to become the new 'boss of bosses'. On February 26, 1930, Gaetano Reina was murdered and Masseria appointed Joseph Pinzolo as the new boss of the Reina family. During the war Profaci remained neutral, while he secretly supported Maranzano.

The Castellammarese War ended when Charles "Lucky" Luciano, a Masseria lieutenant, betrayed him to Maranzano. Luciano set up the murder of Masseria on April 15, 1931 Maranzano then became the new Capo di tutti capi in the United States. Within a few months, Maranzano and Luciano were plotting to kill each other. On September 10, 1931, Luciano had Maranzano killed and created the Mafia Commission. Now there would be five independent Cosa Nostra families in New York City and twenty one additional families across the United States that were regulated by a supreme Commission in New York. Profaci and Magliocco were confirmed as boss and underboss, respectively, of what was now known as the Profaci crime family.

First Family War

(1960-1963)

Joseph Profaci in 1959

Joseph Profaci had become a wealthy Mafia boss and was known as "the olive-oil and tomato paste king of America". One of Profaci's most unpopular demands was a $25 monthly tribute from every soldier in his family. In the late 1950s, capo Frank "Frankie Shots" Abbatemarco became a problem for Joe Profaci. Abbatemarco controlled a lucrative *policy game* that earned him nearly $2.5 million a year with an average of $7,000 a day in Red Hook, Brooklyn. In early 1959, Abbatemarco, with the support of Gallo brothers and the Garfield Boys, began refusing to pay tribute to Profaci. By late 1959, Abbatemarco's debt had grown to $50,000 and Profaci allegedly ordered Joe Gallo to murder Abbatemarco.

However, other versions of the story indicate that Gallo played no part in this murder. In return for Abbatemarco's murder, Profaci allegedly agreed to give the Gallos control over Abbatemarco's policy game. On November 4, 1959, Frank Abbatemarco walked out of his cousin's bar in Park Slope, Brooklyn and was shot and killed by Joseph Gioielli and another hitman. Profaci then ordered the Gallos to hand over Abbatemaro's son Anthony. The Gallos refused and Profaci refused to give them the policy game. This was the start of the first family war. The Gallo brothers and the Garfield boys (led by Carmine Persico) were aligned against Profaci and his loyalists.

On February 27, 1961 the Gallos kidnapped four of Profaci's top men: underboss Magliocco, Frank Profaci (Joe Profaci's brother), capo Salvatore Musacchio and soldier John Scimone. Profaci himself eluded capture and flew to sanctuary in Florida. While holding the hostages, Larry and Albert Gallo sent Joe Gallo to California. Profaci's Consigliere Charles "the Sidge" LoCicero negotiated with the Gallos and all the hostages were released peacefully. However, Profaci had no intention of honoring this peace agreement. On August 20, 1961 Joseph Profaci ordered the murder of Gallo members Joseph "Joe Jelly" Gioielli and Larry Gallo. Gunmen allegedly murdered Gioilli after inviting him to go deep sea fishing. Gallo survived a strangulation attempt in the Sahara club of East Flatbush by Carmine Persico and Salvatore "Sally" D'Ambrosio after a police officer intervened. The Gallos then began calling Persico *"The Snake"*; he had betrayed them, the war continued on resulting in nine murders and three disappearances.

In late November 1961, Joe Gallo was sentenced to seven-to-fourteen years in prison for murder. In 1962, Joe Profaci died of cancer, leaving Joe Magliocco, his longtime underboss, as the new boss. The war continued on between the two factions. In 1963, Carmine Persico survived a car bombing and his enforcer Hugh McIntosh was shot in the groin as he attempted kill Larry Gallo. On May 19, 1963, a Gallo hit team shot Carmine Persico multiple times, but Persico survived.

In 1963, Magliocco and Bonanno boss Joseph Bonanno hatched an audacious plan to murder bosses Carlo Gambino, Tommy Lucchese, Stefano Magaddino and Frank DeSimone and take over the Mafia Commission. Joseph Magliocco gave the murder contact to Joseph Colombo. Colombo either feared for his life, or sensed an opportunity for advancement, and instead reported the plot to The Commission. The Commission, realizing that Bonanno was the real mastermind, ordered both Magliocco and Bonanno to appear for a Mob trial. Bonanno went into hiding, but a badly shaken Magliocco appeared and confessed everything. He was fined $43,000 and forced into retirement.

Colombo and Italian American Civil Rights League

The Commission rewarded Colombo for his loyalty by awarding him the Profaci family, which he renamed the Colombo family. The 41-year-old Colombo was the youngest boss in New York at the time. He was also the first boss to have been born and raised in the United States.

Along with former Gallo crew member Nicholas Bianco and New England family boss Raymond Patriarca, Colombo was able to end the war. As a reward for his loyalty, Bianco was made into the Colombo family. As boss, Colombo brought peace and stability to the broken crime family. However, some Cosa Nostra bosses viewed Colombo as Carlo Gambino's "puppet boss" and felt he never deserved the title. Colombo's leadership was never challenged due to his support from Carlo Gambino. In 1968, Gallo crew leader Larry Gallo died of cancer.

In 1969, Colombo founded the *Italian-American Civil Rights League*, dedicated to fighting discrimination against Italian-Americans. Many mobsters disapproved of the

League because it brought unwanted public attention to the Cosa Nostra. Colombo ignored their concerns and continued gaining support for his league. On July 28, 1970, Colombo held the first league demonstration, a big success. In 1971, months before the second demonstration, the other New York bosses ordered their men to stay away from the demonstration and not support Colombo's cause. In a sign that the New York bosses had turned on Colombo, the league's chief organizer, chief organizer Gambino family capo Joseph DeCicco, resigned ostensibly due to ill health. In 1971, Joe Gallo was also released from prison. At the time of his release, Gallo said the 1963 peace agreement did not apply to him because he was in prison when it was negotiation.

Second Family War
(1971-1975)

The Rally

Columbus Circle

On June 28, 1971, tens of thousands of people converged on Manhattans Columbus Circle for the second annual Italian-American Civil Rights League rally. Police barricades rerouted traffic away from the event. On an outdoor stage festooned with red, white, and blue fringed streamers, prominent politicians and local celebrities gathered to lend their support. Red, white, and green flags of Italy were unfurled beside the Stars and Stripes. Television cameramen and newspaper photographers shouldered their way through the crowd to get as close to the podium as possible. Proud Italian-Americans from all over the New York metropolitan area gathered to voice their opposition to what they considered government prejudice against their people. They had a particular beef with the FBI. They felt that all Italian-Americans were being tarred with the Mafia brush. Just because a few Italians had established La Cosa Nostra, they certainly weren't all criminals, but the FBI, they claimed, treated them that way.

The crowd cheered when they spotted Joseph Colombo, the founder of the Italian-American Civil Rights League, emerging from his car and making his way through the throng on foot. Oddly enough, Joe Colombo was the reigning boss of the New York crime family that bore his name. For some inexplicable reason, the leagues supporters didn't see the irony.

Joseph Colombo

Colombo had started the league the year before to retaliate against what he considered unfair harassment from the FBI. On April 30, 1970, Colombo's son Joseph Jr. had been arrested for melting down quarters, dimes, and nickels for their silver content, hoping to earn more than the face value of the coins.

As mob expert Jerry Capeci points out, the arrest was a pressure tactic aimed at the young man's father, but Joe Colombo cried foul and impetuously struck back by sending a gang of his men to picket FBI headquarters in Manhattan.

But picketing alone wasn't enough for Colombo. He soon declared that he was forming the Italian-American Civil Rights League to address the issue of discrimination against his people. To the amazement of law-enforcement officials, thousands of law-abiding Italian-Americans took up the cry, sending in their ten-dollar membership fees to the organization in droves. Fearing reprisals from Italian-American voters, local politicians voiced their support. Within a matter of weeks, the league became a force of nature.

Fifty thousand people attended the first rally at Columbus Circle on June 29, 1970. The mob ordered the docks closed for the day so that union members could attend. Stores in Italian neighborhoods around the city also closed in honor of the occasion. The huge outpouring of popular support for the league had its effect. United States Attorney General John Mitchell and New York Governor Nelson Rockefeller declared that the term Mafia would no longer be used within their jurisdictions.

The league named Joe Colombo its Man of the Year in May of that year, even though in March he had been slapped with a two-and-a-half-year prison sentence for lying on his application for a real-estate brokers license. The sentence was delayed pending appeal, and Colombo stepped up his efforts to promote the League. He even appeared on the Dick Cavett Show, a popular late-night television talk show, to discuss anti-Italian-American discrimination. Some of the bosses of the other families were not pleased. This kind of deliberate self-exposure was unheard of for a Mafia chief. Not even the egomaniacal John Gotti would have considered this kind of publicity during his reign as boss of the Gambino Family in the late 80s and early 90s.

By the time the second annual rally rolled around, Joe Colombo, the self-appointed civil rights leader, was walking on thin ice. As he made his way through the crowd on that summer day in 1971, he undoubtedly realized that he had ruffled some feathers, but apparently he didn't know how badly he had ruffled them. The knives were already out.

"Vegetabled"

After the first Italian-American Civil Rights League rally in 1970, Joe Colombo was able to convince many of his fellow bosses and their capos to contribute to his cause. How else would he have gotten the docks to close down for the event? But on December 16, 1970, FBI agents arrested Colombo soldier Rocco Miraglia and searched the briefcase he was carrying. According to *The Complete Idiots Guide to the Mafia*, the special agents found a list of names or nicknames and dollar amounts.

Colombo, who was with Miraglia when he was arrested, appeared before a federal grand jury and was questioned about the list. Rather than pleading the Fifth the way a gangster normally would, Colombo, the civil-rights leader, declared that these dollar amounts were contributions he had raised for the league. Carl, he testified, was boss Carlo Gambino. Next to his name on the list was written 30,000. No doubt Gambino and all the other mobsters on that list wished Colombo hadn't been so forthcoming. The mobs initial support for Colombo's league soon dried up. The bosses felt that he had become too public, and in the mob, that was never good for business.

Joe and Larry Gallo

Joe Colombo also faced serious opposition within his own family. The Gallo brothers - Larry, Albert, and the notorious Crazy Joey - had been chafing under the family's leadership for years and had already tried to take over the family in the early sixties. Joey Gallo had just been released from state prison in February 1971 after serving a nine-year stint, and his bitter feelings about the family leadership hadn't changed. Gallo and his brothers had long felt that they deserved a bigger piece of the pie for their efforts, and they'd proven in the past that they were ready, willing, and able to go to war to get what they wanted. The brothers also had a powerful ally in Genovese capo Vincent Chin Gigante, who would one day become boss of his family.

As Joe Colombo muscled his way through the crowd in Columbus Circle to get to the stage, three gunshots suddenly rang out. People ducked, yelled in panic, and ran for shelter. Police officers fought the stampede to get to the source of the trouble. They found Joe Colombo lying on the pavement, blood streaming from three head wounds. A black man holding a pistol stood over him.

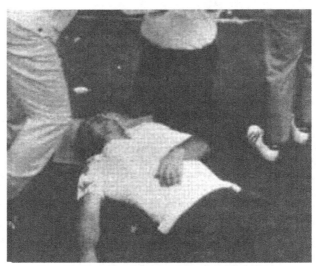

Joe Colombo shot by Jerome Johnson

The police grabbed the man, but as they attempted to restrain him, a loyal Colombo retainer pulled a gun and put three bullets into the man's back, killing him on the spot. Police later learned that the man who shot Colombo was a street hustler named Jerome Johnson who had somehow obtained press credentials from the league. Suspicion immediately fell on Joey Gallo, who had a reputation for doing deals with African-American criminals. Gallo felt that the mob could only benefit from cooperating with black crime groups, but many mobsters didn't like his fraternizing with them.

Jerome Johnson

But police investigations and internal mob inquiries found no connection between Gallo and Jerome Johnson, nor were they able to prove that the gunman had been hired by Carlo Gambino or any other Mafia boss who had a bone to pick with Colombo. Johnson was apparently a crazed lone gunman.

Joey Gallo

Colombo did not die of his wounds. He remained in a coma
for the rest of his life, or, as Joey Gallo characteristically
put it, "he was vegetabled." The shooting of Joe Colombo
was just one chapter in the violent, strife-ridden history of
the Colombo Family, a saga that begins with one of the
most despised mob bosses in the history of the American
Mafia.

The Olive Oil King

Joe Profaci

Joe Profaci, the first and longest reigning boss of the Profaci Family, was hated by his men. As soon as Joe Colombo took his place after his death, the family was almost immediately re-christened the Colombo Family in an effort to erase the memory of his stingy, iron-handed tenure on the throne. Profaci's legitimate business, importing olive oil and tomato paste, earned him the nickname the Olive Oil King, but this business was only a small fraction of his empire.

According to Carl Sifakis in *The Mafia Encyclopedia,* Profaci lived in a huge mansion on a 328-acre estate on Long Island, which boasted a hunting lodge and its own private airport. But while other bosses were often generous with their wealth, Profaci was a skinflint who taxed his men for the right to be in his family.

On top of the usual percentage that a mob boss is entitled to, Profaci charged an additional tax on all criminal activities pursued by his men. Each family member also had to pay dues of $25 a month. Many of Profaci's wiseguys complained behind his back that he was just another mean, tight-fisted Moustache Pete, but Profaci saw himself as a traditionalist who lived by the code of the original Sicilian Mafia.

Profaci was a clever survivor who managed to steer clear of the upheaval of the Castellammarese War in 1931, keeping his family intact while the young Turks, led by Lucky Luciano, were carving up the remains of Salvatore Maranzano's family. The Profaci Family, which was based in Brooklyn and parts of Staten Island, pursued the usual mob enterprises - labor rackets, gambling, hijacking, loan sharking, and extortion, later adding heroin importation to its portfolio. Profaci maintained a close alliance with Bonanno Family boss Joseph Bonanno, and together they were powerful enough to scare off the other encroaching New York families.

Profaci ruled his family for three decades without a serious challenge to his leadership. But by the beginning of the 1960s, the bosses of the Gambino, Lucchese, and Genovese Families were ready for a shift in the power alignment in New York. The Profaci-Bonanno alliance had become an 800-pound gorilla, frequently getting in their way. As mob expert Jerry Capeci points out, Carlo Gambino, who sought out allies among Profaci's men, fomented trouble from within.

The Gallo brothers - Lawrence, Albert, and Joey along with their crew from the Red Hook section of Brooklyn had been dissatisfied with Profaci's leadership for some time.

They scratched out a living with their rackets, but because Profaci always took a big chunk of their profits, they felt that they weren't getting ahead. They were particularly bitter about the Profaci-ordered execution of fellow crew-member Frank Frankie Shots Abbatemarco. Profaci felt that Frankie Shots, a numbers banker, had become disloyal and disrespectful in withholding tribute to the boss. The Gallos didn't dispute the charge, but felt that the punishment far outweighed the gravity of the crime.

Joseph Magliocco

By February 1961, the Gallo crew had finally had enough. In a bold move, they kidnapped several prominent members of the family, including longtime underboss Joseph Magliocco and capo Joe Colombo. The Gallos then sent word to Profaci that they wanted some changes made in the way profits were divvied up. Profaci sent his *consigliere* Charles The Sidge Locicero to negotiate with them.

After weeks of negotiations, the two sides came to an agreement, and the hostages were released. Everyone was apparently happy with the outcome.

Larry Gallo

But six months later, Profaci retaliated. One of the hostages, soldier John Scimone, lured Larry Gallo to a bar in Brooklyn, where two thugs threw a rope around his neck and started to choke him. They threatened to kill him if he didn't call his brothers and tell them to come to the bar. Larry Gallo knew he and his brothers would all be dead if he did that, so he refused to cooperate. The rope was pulled tighter, and Gallo would have been a goner if a policeman hadn't suddenly walked in. The front door of the bar had been left ajar, and because it was a Sunday, and blue laws demanded that all commercial establishments close shop on Sundays, the cop came in to investigate.

Scimone and his thugs ran for the door. The cops partner tried to stop them, but one of the hoods shot him in the face. They escaped in a waiting Cadillac.

The Gallos then learned that Profaci's men had killed their chief enforcer, Joseph Joe Jelly Gioelli, a few days earlier. The Gallo crew lashed out, taking potshots at Profaci loyalists wherever they found them. He police raided the Gallo crew's headquarters in Brooklyn, hoping to head off an all-out war within the family. The violence subsided, but the bitterness festered.

Profaci's troubles weren't relegated to internal matters. In early 1962, Carlo Gambino and Tommy Lucchese went before the Mafia Commission and proposed that Profaci retire as boss for the good of his family and the mob in general. Joe Bonanno vehemently objected to such a move, fearing that he'd lose his most important ally. The Commission decided not to decide in this matter, and it became a moot point when Profaci succumbed to cancer on June 6, 1962.

Joseph Magliocco

Profaci's underboss, Joseph Magliocco, was quickly installed as boss, which did not please Lucchese and Gambino. From all indications, Magliocco would faithfully carry on with Profaci's policies, including the close alliance with Joe Bonanno. For that reason, the old boss's enemies automatically became the new boss's enemies.

Trouble and More Trouble

Carmine "Junior" Persico

Joe Magliocco must have had days when he regretted taking over as boss of Profaci's family. The Gallo crew still wasn't happy, and they came at him with a vengeance, determined to bring him down. Hoping to weaken Magliocco hold on the family, they targeted his strongest men, particularly the fierce Carmine Junior Persico. Persico's car was bombed in 1963, but he escaped with only minor injuries. On May 19 of that year, he was shot in the face, hand, and shoulder, according to mob expert Jerry Capeci, in a drive-by shooting orchestrated by the Gallos. Persico was reportedly so tough he spat out one of the bullets that entered his face. In another incident, Persico's chief enforcer, Hugh McIntosh, a giant of a man who wore a size 52 suit, was ambushed and shot but managed to survive.

But the Gallo revolt came to an abrupt halt in the fall of 1963, when two key crew members were murdered and seventeen others were indicted on a variety of racketeering charges. With Joey Gallo already almost two years into a lengthy prison sentence, the Gallo crew just didn't have the manpower to keep the fight going.

Stefano Magaddino

Magliocco may have been relieved to have the pesky Gallo crew off his back, but his real troubles were just beginning. He had inherited Joe Profaci's alliance with the Bonanno Family, but he was an indecisive leader and unfortunately for him took his cues from the ambitious Joe Bonanno. Before Profaci died, he and Bonanno had been plotting the assassination of their chief nemeses, bosses Carlo Gambino, Tommy Lucchese, and Stefano Magaddino of the Buffalo Family (who also happened to be Bonannos cousin). Bonannos goal was to get rid of his enemies and install himself as *capo di tutti capi*, boss of all bosses and head of the Commission. Following Profaci's wishes, Magliocco went along with the plot. Bonanno gave Magliocco the task of having Gambino and Lucchese whacked, and Magliocco passed the contract on to one of his most loyal hit men, Joe Colombo. Magliocco was confident that Colombo would get the job done.

But Colombo had a mind of his own, and he could see which way the wind was blowing. After assessing the situation, he decided that Bonanno was too power-hungry, and his attempt to take over the Commission would ultimately fail, leaving the Profaci Family holding the bag. So instead of carrying out the executions, Colombo informed Lucchese and Gambino of the conspiracy. They in turn went to the Commission and demanded justice.

The Commission did not want to see another Castellammarese War, so they exercised their regulatory powers and summoned Magliocco and Bonanno to appear before them. Bonanno defied the order and went into hiding. Magliocco obeyed the order and admitted his part in the conspiracy. The Commission took pity on him, knowing that the devious Bonanno had to have been the driving force behind the plot. Magliocco was fined $50,000 and forced to retire. They spared his life, but Magliocco had a heart attack and died a few months later.

Carlo Gambino

At the suggestion of Carlo Gambino, Joe Colombo was rewarded for his part in thwarting the conspiracy and made the new boss of the Profaci Family. Gambino would come to regret that endorsement when Colombo and his love of publicity threw an unwanted spotlight on the organized-crime underworld.

Star Power

As a young man, Joe Colombo made his mark as part of Joe Profaci's elite execution squad, a five-man hit team that included Larry and Joey Gallo. When you killed with the Gallo boys, Carl Sifakis writes in *The Mafia Encyclopedia,* you killed with the best. In addition to his hit-man duties, Colombo initially worked as an enforcer on the docks, then moved up to running gambling dens, hijacking, and loan-sharking. But perhaps what formed his thinking more than any of his criminal experiences was the gangland slaying of his father, Anthony Colombo, who was found garroted in his car along with his girlfriend. Joe Colombo knew firsthand how quickly a wiseguy can fall out of favor and be exterminated. Colombo was probably thinking of his father's fate when he decided that siding with Carlo Gambino and Tommy Lucchese was a better bet than following his own boss Joe Magliocco and the power-mad Joe Bonanno.

Sam DeCavalcante

In January 1964, at age 41, Colombo became one of the youngest men ever to take over a mob family.

Many within the Mafia welcomed the regime change, but some had their doubts about Colombo's competence. What experience has he got? New Jersey boss Sam The Plumber DeCavalcante complained in a conversation taped by the FBI. What does he know? But as Colombo settled into his position, some felt that he was the most progressive mob leader to come down the pike in some years. Others felt he was a self-centered showboat who sported excessively expensive suits and enjoyed being covered by the press.

When he formed the Italian American Civil Rights League, his fellow mobsters didn't know what to think. On one hand, they agreed with his cause, believing that all Italian-Americans were unfairly targeted by law enforcement simply because of their heritage. But on the other hand, they traditionally thrived in the shadows away from public scrutiny. Colombo, they felt, was drawing too much attention to them. After an initial showing of support, mobsters tried to distance themselves from him, especially after the FBI discovered the damning list of mob donors.

The attempt on his life at the league rally in 1971 was too public to have been a Mafia hit. Despite the finger-pointing by the police, it just wasn't the way the mob did things. They would have chosen an isolated spot late at night and away from witnesses, not unlike the way his father was killed. Nevertheless, Colombo's incapacitation was not an unwelcome event to those who felt he had stepped dangerously out of bounds.

Colombo survived the shooting, but just barely. Brain-dead and unresponsive, he lived seven more years, finally dying in 1978. During that time, the Colombo Family closed ranks and chose not to reveal the identity of their new boss. The FBI worked for three years to find out who he was.

Finally, they discovered that the new boss was Thomas DiBella, a wiseguy who hardly registered on their radar screens. With only one conviction for bootlegging in 1932, they had no idea how important DiBella was in the family hierarchy.

Keeping things quiet was a good idea, but no sooner did one mob star get vegetabled than another one found the spotlight, and this one threatened to shine brighter than even Joe Colombo.

The Return of Crazy Joey

Joey Gallo

The Colombo Family's attempts to keep a low profile were threatened by the release of Crazy Joey Gallo from prison in 1971. The Crazy nickname was misleading. Mob traditionalists called him crazy because his ideas were so progressive. He saw the future of organized crime, and it went far beyond the Little Italy social clubs and Brooklyn hangouts of the Italian-American gangsters. There was money to be made in Harlem and other black neighborhoods, and he wanted the mob to be in on it. Gallo advocated forming partnerships with black gangsters, reasoning that they would give the Mafia inroads into rackets they otherwise couldn't touch.

Gallo had gained some culture during his stint at New York States Greenhaven Prison. He devoured books and newspapers and took up painting. He spoke authoritatively about the great artists he'd studied. Shortly after he returned from prison, a movie based on Jimmy Breslin's novel *The Gang That Couldn't Shoot Straight* was released. The novel and film were a comic take on Gallos Brooklyn crew. The fictional gang kept a lion in their basement to scare tardy payments out of loan-sharking customers. The Gallo crew actually did keep a pet lion that they routinely introduced to their habitual deadbeats. Joey Gallo didn't find the movie very funny, and was particularly upset with the portrayal of Kid Sally Palumbo, the character supposedly based on him. The actor who played Kid Sally was Jerry Orbach (who would later play Detective Lenny Briscoe on the long-running *Law & Order* television series). Gallo wanted to set Orbach straight on how real mobsters lived, so he invited the actor and his wife to dinner. Orbach accepted the invitation and was so impressed with Gallos knowledge of books and art that they eventually became friends. Orbach introduced Gallo to several of his show-business friends. Soon Gallo was seen around town, hobnobbing with celebrities. He even moved from Brooklyn to Greenwich Village to be closer to his new crowd.

Jerry Orbach

On April 7, 1972, Gallo was celebrating his birthday at the Copacabana night club with a group of friends that included Orbach, comedian David Steinberg, and columnist Earl Wilson. The party finally disbanded in the wee hours, and Gallo, his bodyguard, and four women went to Little Italy in downtown Manhattan, looking for a restaurant that was open. They found their way to Umberto's Clam House on Mulberry Street. Gallo and his bodyguard, Pete the Greek Diapoulas, made the mistake of sitting with their backs to the door, figuring they were safe on Mafia holy ground. But a gunman with a .38 walked in and started shooting. Women screamed. Patrons hit the floor. Gallo assumed that he was the intended target, so he got up from the table and ran for the door; drawing fire away from the innocent. The killer trained his gun on Gallo and kept shooting. Gallo made it outside to the sidewalk, where he collapsed and died next to his Cadillac.

Like Joe Colombo, Joey Gallo learned the hard way that the mob has no use for the limelight.

Third Family War
(1991-1993)

Orena, an ambitious capo from Cedarhurst, was initially content with serving as acting boss. By 1990, however, Orena had come to believe Persico was out of touch and causing the family to miss out on lucrative opportunities. He was also alarmed at Persico's plans for a made-for-television biography, fearing that prosecutors could use it as evidence in the same way they had used Joe Bonanno's tell-all book as evidence in the Commission Trial. He therefore decided to take over the family himself. Using his strong ties to Gambino boss John Gotti, Orena petitioned the Mafia Commission to declare him the official boss of the Colombo family. Unwilling to cause more conflict, the Commission refused. Orena then instructed consigliere Carmine Sessa to poll the capos on whether Orena should become boss. Instead, Sessa alerted Persico that Orena was staging a palace coup. On June 21, 1991, an enraged Persico sent gunmen under Sessa's leadership to murder Orena at his house. However, Orena managed to escape before the gunmen could strike. The third Colombo war had begun.

Twelve people, including three innocent bystanders, died in this gang war. More than 80 made members and associates from both sides of the Colombo family were convicted, jailed or indicted. These included Persico's brother Theodore "Teddy" Persico and his son Alphonse Persico, DeRoss, and Orena's two sons, Victor, Jr. Orena and John Orena. While both sides appealed to the Commission for help, the war continued.

In November 18, 1991, when two carloads of Orena supporters ambushed Persico capo Greg Scarpa Sr. in Brooklyn as he drove his daughter and granddaughter home. Hit men ran from their vehicles with guns drawn and converged on Scarpa's car. But Scarpa, one of the toughest gangsters the mob has ever seen, hit the accelerator and made a run for it, crashing into anything that got in his way. Fenders crunched and bullets flew. A few bystanders were injured, but Scarpa and his loved ones escaped unharmed. After the incident, Scarpa, who had been diagnosed with AIDS in 1986 after receiving a tainted blood transfusion from a member of his crew, entered the fray like a wild man. He had nothing to lose.

Scarpa and his relatives managed to escape. This attempt on his life forced him to reach out to the other families for help. He renewed his petition to the Commission to dethrone Persico and legitimize his position as undisputed boss. Sessa appealed to the Commission on behalf of Persico, portraying Orena as an upstart who was betraying his boss.

(Interestingly, Scarpa had been a secret FBI informer for 30 years, playing both sides of the fence to his own advantage. As for his legendary toughness, he matched Carmine Persico, who had once spit out a bullet fired into his face. In 1992, Scarpa took a bullet in the eye during a shootout. According to Jerry Capeci, Scarpa drove himself home, poured himself a Scotch, and called the police. He lost the eye.)

Five days after their attempt on Scarpa's life, Orena supporters came back hard, gunning down Henry Hank the Bank Smurra outside a doughnut shop in Brooklyn. This hit team was led by William Wild Bill Cutolo.

The Colombo Family fell into chaos when the aging and ailing Thomas DiBella voluntarily stepped down as boss. His logical successor was the family's most powerful capo, Carmine Junior Persico, but Persico had faced a relentless onslaught of prosecutions that sent him to prison for ten of the 13 years prior to 1985, according to Carl Sifakis in *The Mafia Encyclopedia*. Still, he managed to maintain his position as boss while incarcerated, empowering his brother Alphonse and Gennaro Jerry Lang Langella to carry out his orders. During this period, the family concentrated their efforts on narcotics and labor racketeering.

The war continued until 1992, when Orena was convicted on massive RICO charges and sentenced to 100 years in prison. As it turned out, the real winners in the war were federal prosecutors. They had initially made little headway in their efforts to undermine the gang. As the war raged, though, at least 12 members turned informer, mostly to save their lives. The highest-profile member to flip was the consigliere, Sessa. With their help, 58 soldiers and associates—42 from the Persico faction and 16 from the Orena faction—were sent to prison. George Stamboulidis, who prosecuted most of the cases arising from the war, later said that the two years of bloodletting helped prosecutors destroy the family from within. He credited the large number of informers with helping them to build big cases sooner than they would have otherwise been able to. Raab later wrote that Persico's attempts to keep control of the family from prison nearly destroyed it.

While the Colombo war raged, the Commission refused to allow any Colombo member to sit on the Commission and considered dissolving the family. Lucchese underboss Anthony Casso proposed to merge the family with his own to end the war, while in 2000 plans were proposed to split its manpower and resources among the remaining families.

In 2002, with the help of Bonanno family boss Joseph Massino, the Commission finally allowed the Colombos to rejoin them.

The family after Third Colombo War

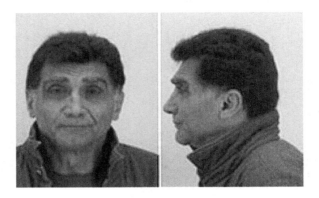

Mugshot of Ralph DeLeo

With Orena out of the picture, Persico designated his son Alphonse as acting boss. "Little Allie Boy" officially took over after his 1995 parole, but didn't rule for long. In 1999, he was arrested in Fort Lauderdale after being caught in possession of a pistol and shotgun; as a convicted felon he was barred from carrying guns. Shortly afterward, he ordered the murder of underboss William "Wild Bill" Cutolo, a supporter of Orena during the Third Colombo War. Cutolo's son, vowing revenge, offered to wear a wire and pose as a prospective Colombo associate. Based on evidence from this wire, Little Allie Boy was indicted on RICO charges. Realizing he stood no chance of acquittal, he pleaded guilty to the state charges in February 2000 and to the RICO charges in December 2001. In 2004, Alphonse Persico and Underboss John "Jackie" DeRoss were indicted for the Cutolo murder. In December 2007, both men were convicted and sentenced to life in prison.

Family consigliere Joel "Joe Waverly" Cacace took over running the family until 2003 when he was imprisoned on murder and racketeering charges.

The family then came under the influence of Thomas "Tommy Shots" Gioeli, who took over as street boss. In June 2008, Gioeli, underboss John "Sonny" Franzese, former consigliere Joel Cacace, captain Dino Calabro, soldier Dino Saracino and several other members and associates were indicted on multiple racketeering charges which included loan sharking, extortion and three murders dating back to the Colombo Wars. If convicted, they are all facing life sentences.

After Gioeli was imprisoned, Ralph F. DeLeo, who operated from Boston, Massachusetts, became the family's street boss. On December 17, 2009, the FBI charged DeLeo and Colombo family members with drug trafficking, extortion and loansharking in Massachusetts, Rhode Island, New York, Florida and Arkansas.

Behind Bars

Ruling the family from his federal prison cell in Lompoc, California, Carmine Persico continued to pull strings in the hope of getting his son Alphonse on the throne. The college-educated Allie Persico was scheduled to be released from prison in May 1993, after which he would have taken over as boss. But the government had other ideas. They charged him with crimes relating to his participation in the Colombo War, hoping to keep him locked up, but in August 1994, he was found not guilty.

Andrew Russo

Perhaps not wanting to risk a parole violation for consorting with known criminals, Alphonse Persico laid low while one of his father's cousins, Andrew Russo, took over as acting boss in 1996. Three years later, Russo was tried and convicted on racketeering and jury-tampering charges.

Alphonse took his place as acting boss, but within a few months he was arrested by the Coast Guard off the Florida Keys for gun possession. A search of his speedboat, the Lookin Good, yielded a loaded pistol and shotgun. In 2000, he was tried on the gun charges and sentenced to 18 months in prison.

According to Ganglandnews.com, Alphonse Persico threw in the towel on December 20, 2001, pleading guilty to loan-sharking, money-laundering, and racketeering charges. A plea-bargain deal called for him to pay the government $1 million and serve 13 years in prison. Persico still faces the possibility of execution if the government tries him for the murder of Wild Bill Cutolo.

In January 2005, *New York* Magazine cited Carmine Junior Persico as the boss of the Colombo Family, with John Jackie DeRoss as his underboss, Joel Joe Waverly Cacace as his *consigliere,* and Thomas Tommy Shots Gioeli as his street boss. According to the magazine, Gioeli has been able to bridge the gap that exists between mobsters who were shooting at each other a decade ago. But given their history, one has to wonder if the wounds of the Colombo War will ever heal.

Historical leadership

Boss (official and acting)

The Boss (also sometimes called *Godfather* or *Don*) is the head of his own family. He makes all the major decisions within the organization. The Boss, Underboss, and Consigliere are the only men allowed to induct an associate into the family. If the Boss is incarcerated or debilitated, he chooses an Acting Boss to enforce his decisions.

1928–1962 — Joseph Profaci – died of natural causes

1962–1963 — Joseph Magliocco – forced to retire by Mafia Commission

1963–1971 — Joseph Colombo – paralyzed by assassination attempt

Acting 1971–1972 — Joseph Yacovelli– fled, after the murder of Joe Gallo

Acting - 1972–1973 – Vincenzo "Vincent" Aloi – imprisoned

Acting - 1973 — Joseph "Joey" Brancato– imprisoned

1973–present — Carmine "Junior" Persico – imprisoned 1973–1979, 1981–1984, 1985–present

Acting - 1973–1979 — Thomas DiBella– stepped down, became consigliere

Acting - 1981–1983 — Alphonse "Allie Boy" Persico – Carmine Persico's brother; fugitive 1980–1987, imprisoned

Acting - 1983–1984 — Gennaro "Jerry Lang" Langella – imprisoned

Acting - 1985–1987 — Anthony "Scappy" Scarpati – imprisoned

Acting - 1987–1991 — Vittorio "Vic" Orena – imprisoned sentenced to life

Acting - 1991–1993 — *Vacant* – disputed leadership during the third war

Acting - 1994–1996 — Andrew "Andy Mush" Russo – imprisoned March 1997

Acting - 1996–present — Alphonse "Little Allie Boy" Persico – Carmine Persico's son; imprisoned 2000–present

Street Boss

1987 — *Ruling Panel* – Benedetto Aloi, Vincent "Jimmy" Angelino and Joseph T. Tomasello – disbanded September 1987

1991–1993 — Joseph T. Tomasello

1993–1994 — *Ruling Panel* – Joseph T. Tomasello, Theodore "Teddy" Persico and Joseph Baudanza – disbanded 1994

1994–1996 — Alphonse "Little Allie Boy" Persico – became acting boss

1996–1999 — Andrew "Andy Mush" Russo – imprisoned

2000–2003 — Joel "Joe Waverly" Cacace – imprisoned January 2003

2003–2008 — Thomas "Tommy Shots" Gioeli – imprisoned June 2008

2008–2009 — Ralph F. DeLeo– operated from New England, imprisoned December 2009

2009–2010 — *Ruling Panel* – Theodore N. Persico, Jr. (jailed) and others

2010–present — Andrew "Andy Mush" Russo – jailed January 2011

Underboss

(Official and acting)

1928–1962 — Joseph "Joe Malyak" Magliocco – promoted to Boss

1962–1963 — Salvatore "Sally the Sheik" Musacchio – brother-in-law to Joseph Magliocco

1963–1967 — John "Sonny" Franzese– imprisoned

1967–1971 — Charles "Charlie Lemons" Mineo– stepped down

1971–1973 — Sebastian "Buster" Aloi

1973–1977 — Anthony "Tony Shots" Abbatemarco – fled

Acting 1973–1975 — Andrew "Andy Mush" Russo

1977–1981 — Alphonse "Allie Boy" Persico – Carmine Persico's brother; promoted to Acting Boss

1981–1994 — Gennaro "Jerry Lang" Langella – promoted to Acting Boss

Acting 1983–1987 — John "Sonny" Franzese – imprisoned

Acting 1987— Benedetto "Benny" Aloi

Acting 1991–1993 — *Vacant* — disputed leadership during the third war

1994–1999 — Joel "Joe Waverly" Cacace – became Consigliere

Acting 1993–1999 — Benedetto "Benny" Aloi

1999 — William "Wild Bill" Cutolo – murdered 1999

1999–2004 — John DeRoss – imprisoned life sentence

Acting 2001–2003 — Thomas Gioeli – promoted to Acting Boss

2004–present — John "Sonny" Franzese – On January 14, 2011, was sentenced to eight years in prison.

Acting 2008–2009 — Theodore "Skinny Teddy" Persico, Jr. – Theodore Persico's son; joined the ruling panel

Acting 2009–2011 — Benjamin "The Claw" Castellazzo – jailed January 2011

Consigliere

(Official and acting)

1931–1954 — Salvatore Profaci – Joseph Profaci's brother; died

1954–1963 — Carlaggero "Charles the Sidge" LoCicero – murdered 1968

1963–1969 — Benedetto D'Alessandro

1970–1973 — Joseph "Joey Yack" Yacovelli – became Acting Boss 1971

1973–1977 — Alphonse "Allie Boy" Persico – Carmine Persico's brother; promoted to Underboss

1977–1983 — Thomas "Old Man" DiBella– stepped down

1983–1988 — Alphonse "Allie Boy" Persico – Carmine Persico's brother; died in 1989

Acting 1983–1986 — Thomas "Old Man" DiBella – retired

Acting - 1987–1988 — Vincent "James" Angellino

1988–1993 — Carmine Sessa

Acting - 1988–1991 — Benedetto "Benny" Aloi – promoted to Acting Underboss

Acting - 1991–1993 — *Vacant* – disputed leadership during the third war

1993–1999 — Vincenzo "Vinny" Aloi

1999–2008 — Joel "Joe Waverly" Cacace – promoted to Acting Boss

Acting - 2001–2004 — Ralph "Ralphie" Lombardo

Acting - 2004–2008 — Vincenzo "Vinny" Aloi

2008–2011 — Richard "Ritchie Nerves" Fusco – jailed January 2011

2011–present — Thomas "Tom Mix" Farese

Factions of the third war

The Colombo crime family divided into two factions during the third family war (1991 to 1993).

The Persico faction

Boss – Carmine "Junior" Persico

Acting Boss – Joseph T. Tomasello

Underboss – Jerry Langella

Acting Underboss – Joseph "JoJo" Russo

Consigliere – Carmine Sessa

The Orena faction

Boss – Vittorio "Vic" Orena

Underboss – Joseph Scopo

Consigliere – Vincenzo Aloi

Current family members

Administration

Boss Carmine "Junior" Persico – has been boss since 1973. In 1986, Persico was convicted in the Mafia Commission Trial and sentenced to 100 years in federal prison. His projected release date is March 20, 2050.

Acting Boss Alphonse "Little Allie Boy" Persico – is Carmine Persico's son, holding the title of "Acting Boss". In 2009, Alphonse was sentenced to life in prison and is currently in the United States Penitentiary, Florence in Colorado.

Street Boss Andrew "Andy Mush" Russo – is Carmine Persico's cousin. In November 1986, Russo was sentenced to 14 years; he was released on July 29, 1994 under special parole conditions. In August 1999, Russo was convicted of jury tampering and sentenced to 57 months; he was also sentenced to 123 months for both parole violation and his involvement in a racketeering case of a Long Island carting company. In March 2010, after his parole period expired, Russo became Street boss. In January 2011, Russo was indicted on federal racketeering charges. On March 21, 2013, Russo was sentenced to thirty three months for racketeering. He is currently being held at the Brooklyn Metropolitan Detention Center with an unknown projected release date.

Underboss John "Sonny" Franzese – a longtime member of the family. In 2011, Franzese was sentenced to eight years in prison. His projected release date is June 25, 2017.

Acting Underboss Benjamin "The Claw" Castellazzo – on January 20, 2011, Castellazzo was indicted on federal racketeering charges. In September 2011, Castellazzo pleaded guilty to a reduced charge. On January 30, 2013 Castellazzo was sentenced to 63 months. He is currently incarcerated at the Metropolitan Detention Center in Brooklyn with a projected release date of August 16, 2015.

Consigliere Thomas "Tom Mix" Farese – is Carmine Persico's nephew. His wife Suzanne is the daughter of the late Alphonse Persico (Carmine Persico's brother).During the 1970s, Farese moved from Boston to Fort Lauderdale, Florida where he became friends with Colombo mobster Nicholas Forlano. In July 1978, Farese was made into the Colombo family. In 1980, he was convicted of smuggling marijuana and was sentenced to 30 years in prison, he was released in 1994. In 1998, Farese plead guilty to money laundering. On January 5, 2012, Farese was arrested on charges of loansharking and money laundering in South Florida. Prosecutors obtained evidence on Farese through a recording device on government informant Reynold Maragni. On March 22, 2012, Farese was released from jail on $2.5 million bond. During his trial in September the judge allowed Farese lawyer to inspect informant Reynold Maragni's wristwatch that contained secret recording device. In December 2012, Farese was acquitted of all charges

Caporegimes

Brooklyn faction

(*In prison*) Thomas "Tommy Shots" Gioeli – a capo and former Street boss. Gioeli's crew is operating in Brooklyn, Staten Island and Long Island. In June 2008, Gioeli along with John Franzese, Joel Cacace, Dino Calabro, Dino Saracino were indicted on multiple racketeering and murders from the third Colombo family War. In 2011, Gioeli's acting capo Paul Bevacqua became a government informant. As of October 2011, Gioeli is being held at the Metropolitan Detention Center in Brooklyn.

Joseph Baudanza – a capo with operations in Brooklyn, Manhattan and Staten Island. Baudanza along with his brother Carmine and nephew John were arrested and convicted on stock fraud in 2008. Baudanza was released from prison in February 2011.

William "Billy" Russo – a capo and the youngest son of Andrew Russo. His brother Joseph "Jo Jo" Russo died in prison in 2007.

James "Jimmy Green Eyes" Clemenza – a capo operating in Brooklyn. On August 25, 1961 he tried to strangle Larry Gallo with a rope in a Brooklyn bar. In the mid-1990s, Clemenza along with his brother Gerard "Jerry", and brothers Chris and Anthony Colombo, were placed on the "shelf" for backing Orena during the family war. In 1999, Clemenza along with his brother Jerry were under FBI surveillance attending a dinner in a Little Italy restaurant on Mulberry Street with cast members of "The Sopranos".

Long Island faction

Ralph "Ralphie" Lombardo – a capo and former acting consigliere. Lombardo runs bookmaking and loansharking activities on Long Island. In 1975, Lombardo was convicted of conspiracy of selling stock in an automobile leasing company in New Jersey. In 2003, Lombardo was the Consigliere and he was indicted on illegal gambling, loan-sharking and witness tampering. He was released from prison on August 27, 2006. (*In prison*) Michael Uvino – a capo since 2007. Uvino ran his crew from *"The sons of Italy Social Club"* in Hauppauge, Long Island. In 2009, Uvino was sentenced to 10 years for running illegal card games on Long Island and for assaulting two men. His projected release date is May 24, 2016.

Soldiers

Vincenzo "Vinny" Aloi – a former consigliere, semi-retired in 2008, is residing in Florida.

Vincent Langella – the son of Gennaro Langella. In 2001, Langella pled guilty to racketeering conspiracy. On July 3, 2001, he was sentenced to 27 months in prison. Langella was released on April 12, 2005.

Charles "Moose" Panarella – a hitman who spent time in Las Vegas. Declared mentally unfit for trial, under house arrest.

Daniel Persico – the son of Theodore Persico. In March 2000, Daniel was arrested and later convicted on a pump and dump stock scam. He was released from prison on November 14, 2003.

Thomas Petrizzo – a soldier who operated a contracting company in Middlesex, New Jersey.

Imprisoned soldiers

Theodore "Teddy" Persico - brother to Carmine Persico, uncle to Alphonse "Little Allie Boy" Persico, and father to Theodore N. Persico, Jr. Theodore, Sr. has been a capo in Brooklyn since the 1970s. He served on the family ruling panel from the early 1990s until his arrest and conviction. Theodore, Sr.'s projected release date from prison is October 9, 2013.

Theodore N. Persico, Jr. - the son of Theodore Persico. Worked with his cousins Michael Persico and Lawrence Persico. Theodore, Jr. is currently imprisoned awaiting trial.

Ralph F. DeLeo – a soldier and former street boss. DeLeo lived in Somerville, Massachusetts and led the New England faction for family. During the 1990s, while in prison he met Alphonse Persico when he was released in 1997, he was inducted into Colombo crime family. In 2008, DeLeo became Street Boss after Thomas Gioeli was arrested. On December 17, 2009, DeLeo was indicted on racketeering charges from crimes in five different states. He is currently imprisoned with a release date of October 2, 2025.

John "Jackie" DeRoss – a soldier serving life in prison after his 2009 conviction for the 1999 William Cutolo murder. DeRoss is a brother-in-law to Carmine Persico and served as underboss from 1999 to 2004.

Vincent "Chickie" DeMartino - a soldier. In 1993, DeMartino was sentenced to four years in prison on weapons charges. In 1999, Alphonse Persico ordered DeMartino and Thomas Gioeli to murder William Cutolo.

On July 16, 2001, DeMartino and Michael Spataro attempted to murder Joseph Campanella, but failed. In May 2004, Campanella testified against DeMartino. DeMartino has a projected release date of January 1, 2025.

Anthony "Chucky" Russo - a soldier and cousin to William "Billy" Russo. In the 1990s, Anthony Russo worked closely with his now deceased cousin Joseph "JoJo" Russo in Brooklyn and Long Island.

Michael Catapano - a former acting capo and a nephew of John Franzese. Catapano is currently serving a 6½ year prison sentence after pleading guilty to extorting a pizzeria and a gambling club. His projected release date is May 1, 2016.

Associates

Lawrence "Larry" Persico – the son of imprisoned family boss Carmine Persico and brother to Alphonse Persico and Michael Persico. In 2004, Larry was indicted on racketeering charges. His father wrote a letter to the courts defending his son. Lawrence was sentenced on March 11, 2005 and released on December 9, 2005.

Michael Joseph Persico – the son of imprisoned family boss Carmine Persico and brother to Alphonse Persico and Lawrence Persico. In 2010, Michael was accused of racketeering conspiracy involving debris removal contracts for the site of the former World Trade Center. In 2011, Michael was indicted for supplying firearms in the 1993 murder of Joseph Scopo.

Sean Persico – the son of Theodore Persico and brother to Daniel, Frank and Theodore, Jr., Sean was involved in stock scams.

Family crews

The Garfield Boys – was an Italian American street gang that operated in South Brooklyn sections of Red Hook and Gowanus. The gang was headed by future Colombo boss Carmine Persico from the 1950s to the early 1970s.

Controlled unions

N.Y.C. District Council of Carpenters The Colombo and
Genovese families ran the Council from 1991 to 1996,
extorting huge amounts of money from several N.Y.C.
District Council of Carpenters union locals. Colombo capos
Thomas Petrizzo and Vincent "Jimmy" Angellino
controlled Council President Frederick Devine. The two
crime families illegally used the Council to create hundreds
of "no show" absentee jobs for their associates. In 1998,
government witnesses Sammy Gravano and Vincent Cafaro
testified against Devine. He was found guilty of
embezzling union funds and sentenced to 15 months in
prison.

Former members and associates

Richard "Ritchie Nerves" Fusco – a former consigliere. On January 20, 2011, Fusco was indicted on federal racketeering charges. On September 29, 2011, Fusco pleaded guilty to running a shakedown scheme against the Gambino family; he is likely to receive 18 to 24 months in prison. Fusco was incarcerated at the Metropolitan Detention Center in Brooklyn. In September 2013, Fusco died.

Michael "Yuppie Don" Franzese – son of John Franzese. Michael organized a highly lucrative bootleg gasoline racket with the Russian mob. He retired from the crime family during the 1990s.

Joseph "Jo Jo" Russo – the oldest son of Andrew Russo, convicted in 1994 with his cousin Anthony "Chuckie" Russo. Both men received life sentences after former FBI agent Lindley DeVecchio testified against them. In 2007, Joseph Russo died of kidney cancer in prison.

Salvatore "Sally" D'Ambrosio – During the 1960s First Colombo War, D'Ambrosio and future boss Carmine Persico attempted to murder mobster Larry Gallo. D'Ambrosio also participated in the murder of Joseph Gioelli.

Nicholas "Jiggs" Forlano – former capo who ran a loan-sharking operation with Charles "Ruby" Stein. In the 1970s, Forlano moved to Fort Lauderdale, Florida and started operating there. In 1977, Forlano died of a heart attack at the Hialeah race track in Florida.

Frank "Frankie Shots" Abbatemarco – was born in 1899 and grew up in Red Hook, Brooklyn. During the 1950s, Abbatemarco was a powerful capo in Profaci family controlling Red Hook. On November 4, 1959 Abbatemarco was murdered.

Anthony "Big Tony" Peraino – associate who helped finance groundbreaking adult entertainment movie "Deep Throat". Died of natural causes in 1996.

Dominick "Little Dom" Cataldo – died in prison 1990

Ralph "Little Ralphie" Scopo – influential associate who ran Cement Club for family. Died in prison 1993

Ralph Scopo Jr. - son of Ralph Scopo. Died under indictment for extortion in 2013.

Antonio Cottone – deported to Sicily, where he became the Mafia boss of Villabate, the home town for the Profaci family. Cotonne was murdered in 1956.

Benedetto "Benny" Aloi – capo and brother to Vincent Aloi. During the 1990s Third Colombo war, Aloi was Orena's underboss. In 1991, Aloi was convicted in the Windows Case, was released from prison on March 17, 2009. He died on April 7, 2011.

Associates

Frank Persico - the son of Theodore "Teddy" Persico and cousin of acting Colombo boss Alphonse "Allie" Persico. Frank was a stockbroker who was sentenced to five years in prison for a $15 million stock swindle. Frank was released on July 12, 2006; four months later, Frank died of a heart attack.

Hugh "Apples" MacIntosh – an Irish-American enforcer for Carmine Persico during the 1960s. In 1969, MacIntosh was imprisoned on hijacking charges. In 1975, he was released and went on to control several clubs and loan sharking rings for Persico. In 1982, McIntosh was caught bribing an Internal Revenue Service agent for Carmine Persico's early release. McIntosh was imprisoned after the Colombo trial and released on December 31, 1992. MacIntosh was later arrested for meeting with mobster Daniel Persico and was returned to prison. McIntosh died on November 10, 1997.

Charles Ruby Stein – *"loanshark to the stars"*, an associate and business partner to Nicholas Forlano. Stein ran gambling clubs on the Upper West Side of Manhattan. In the early 1970s, mobster Jimmy Coonan became Stein's bodyguard. Stein was murdered in 1977.

Nicholas "Nicky" Bianco – a Gallo crew member, Bianco later joined the Patriarca crime family. Bianco died in prison in 1994.

Gerard Pappa – a family associate who transferred to become a soldier in the Genovese crime family working with Peter Saverio in the New York windows scheme. Was murdered in 1980 by the Cataldo brothers.

Government

informants and witnesses

Members

Paul "Paulie Guns" Bevacqua – former acting capo of the Gieoli crew. In 2011, Bevacqua became a government witness. On November 11, 2011, Bevacqua died.

Rocco Cagno - soldier. His New Jersey home was used for the murder of mobster Vincent Angellino. In the 1990s, Cagno became a government witness and testified against Denis DeLucia and Joseph Lograno

Dino "Big Dino" Calabro – former capo involved in the 1997 murder of New York Police Department (NYPD) officer Ralph Dols. In 2009, Calabro was convicted of murder. On January 26, 2010, Calabro, facing trial for the Dols murder, became a government witness. Calabro is going to testify against mobster Joel Cacace, who allegedly ordered him to murder Dols.

Joseph "Joe Campy" Campanella – former capo. In 2001, after surviving an assassination attempt, Campanella was arrested and became a government witness.

Joseph "Joey Caves" Competiello – former soldier, he was involved in the 1997 murder of NYPD officer Ralph Dols. In 2000, Competiello became a government witness and led the FBI to find the body of Colombo mobster William Cutolo.

Reynold Maragni – a former capo, who ran loansharking and illegal gambling in South Florida. Maragni was arrested during the January 2011 Federal indictments that arrested 127 Mafia members. In December 2011, Maragni wore a wire for the FBI and obtained information about Thomas Gioeli's role in the 1999 murder of William Cutolo. He was dropped from testifying against consigliere Thomas Farese in 2012 for misconduct.

Salvatore "Big Sal" Miciotta - soldier who participated in four murders in 1996 he became a government witness. While in prison Miciotta fought with former Lucchese underboss Anthony Casso.

Anthony "Big Anthony" Russo – former acting capo, not related to Andrew Russo. In 2011, Russo was charged with the 1993 murder of Orena loyalist Joseph Scopo and agreed to be a federal witness.

Gregory Scarpa, Sr. – notorious hitman and FBI informant from the 1970s to 1994. Scarpa, Sr. died in prison from AIDS–related complications.

Carmine Sessa – consigliere and hitman. In 1993, Sessa became a government witness.

Michael "Mickey" Souza - on July 20, 2010, Souza became a government witness and testified against Genovese mobster Anthony Antico.

Frank "Frankie Blue Eyes" Sparaco - soldier. Expected to testify against Michael Persico in the 1992 Devine murder.

John Pate - capo who participated in the 1991 attempted murder of Victor Orena.

Associates

John Franzese, Jr. - son of underboss John Franzese. In 2004, he became a government witness and testified against his father in his 2010 trial.

Kenny "Kenji" Gallo – former associate of Italian-Japanese heritage. worked for the Colombo family before becoming a government witnesses.

Joseph "Joe Pesh" Luparelli – a Colombo associate and bodyguard to Joseph Yacovelli. Luparelli was part of the team that murdered Colombo mobster Joe Gallo. After the Gallo murder, a fearful Luparelli entered the Witness Protection Program and later testified against Yacovelli.

Salvatore "Crazy Sal" Polisi – a former associate of the Colombo and Gambino crime families. Polisi and his friends Dominick and Joseph Cataldo all joined the Mafia. In 1984, Polisi was arrested on narcotics charges and became a government witness. Polisi testified in John Gotti's 1986 trial.

Gambino crime family

The **Gambino crime family** is one of the "Five Families" that dominates organized crime activities in New York City, United States, within the nationwide criminal phenomenon known as the Mafia (or *Cosa Nostra*). The group is named after Carlo Gambino, boss of the family at the time of the McClellan hearings in 1963, when the structure of organized crime first gained public attention. The group's operations extend from New York and the eastern seaboard to California. Its illicit activities include labor and construction racketeering, gambling, loansharking, extortion, money laundering, prostitution, fraud, hijacking, pier thefts, and fencing.

Carlo Gambino

The rise of what for a time was the most powerful crime family in America began in 1957, the day Albert Anastasia was assassinated while sitting in a barber chair at the Park-Sheraton Hotel in Manhattan. Experts believe Carlo Gambino helped orchestrate the hit to take over the family. Gambino partnered with Meyer Lansky to control gambling interests in Cuba. The family's fortunes grew through 1976, when Gambino appointed his brother-in-law, Paul Castellano, as boss. Castellano infuriated upstart capo John Gotti, who orchestrated Castellano's murder in 1985. Gotti's downfall came in 1992, when his underboss Salvatore "Sammy the Bull" Gravano decided to cooperate with the FBI. Gravano's cooperation brought down Gotti, along with most of the top members of the Gambino family. The family is now run by Domenico Cefalu.

Origins

D'Aquila gang

The origins of the Gambino crime family can be traced back to the D'Aquila gang of Manhattan. Salvatore "Toto" D'Aquila was an influential emigrant from Palermo, Sicily who joined the Morello gang of East Harlem. Founded in the 1890s, the Morellos were the first Italian criminal gang in New York. As other gangs formed in New York, they acknowledged Giuseppe Morello as their boss of bosses. In 1906, D'Aquila's name first appeared on police records for running a confidence scam.

In 1910, Giuseppe Morello and his second-in-command, Ignazio Saietta, were sentenced to 30 years in prison for counterfeiting. With the Morello family weakened, D'Aquila used the opportunity to break away from them and form his own gang in East Harlem. D'Aquila quickly used his ties to other Mafia leaders in the United States to create a network of influence and connections and was soon a powerful force in New York.

New York gangs

By 1910, more Italian gangs had formed in New York City. In Brooklyn, Nicola "Cola" Schirò established a gang of Sicilians from Castellammare del Golfo in Sicily. A second Sicilian gang was formed by Alfred Mineo in Brooklyn. Finally, there were two allied Neopolitan Camorra gangs, one on Coney Island and one on Navy Street in Brooklyn, that were run by Pellegrino Morano and Alessandro Vollero.

Giuseppe Masseria

In 1913, Masseria had ruthlessly taken over the Morello Gang, New York's first major Mafia family. Short, stocky, and cold-blooded, Masseria insisted that his underlings call him "Joe the Boss," but he was hardly a beloved leader. Like Nick Morello before him, he was an old-school "Mustache Pete," who ruled with an iron fist and always took the biggest piece of the pie for himself. But in the late 1920s, newly arrived immigrants from the Sicilian town Castellammare del Golfo challenged his control of the New York rackets. Salvatore Maranzano emerged as the boss of these newcomers and thus became Masseria's arch foe. Maranzano's organization established its headquarters in Brooklyn and set up outposts in Buffalo, Cleveland, and Detroit.

In New York, gangsters were forced to take sides. Either they were with Masseria or Maranzano. Neutrality wasn't an option. Masseria had his "young Turks:" Lucky Luciano, Albert Anastasia, Vito Genovese, Frank Costello, Joe Adonis, Willie Moretti, and Carlo Gambino. Maranzano could count on Joe Magliocco, Joe Bonanno, and Joe Profaci as well as "secret defectors" from Masseria's camp, Tommy Lucchese and Tommy Gagliano.

Maranzano was as much a stern "Mustache Pete" as Masseria, and privately the young Turks wished both bosses would go back to Italy. They felt handcuffed by the old-timers' insistence on tradition and impoverished by their bosses' greed. They watched jealously as their rival Irish and Jewish gangs grew fat on the spoils of their wide-ranging criminal activities. Finally fed up, the young Turks secretly formed a third faction, led by Lucky Luciano, who had been running his own rackets behind Masseria's back with Jewish hoodlums Meyer Lansky and Bugsy Siegel, both of whom the anti-Semitic Masseria despised.

In 1917, D'Aquila successfully absorbed the two Camorra gangs. A year earlier, the Camorra had assassinated Nicholas Morello, head of the Morello gang. In response, D'Aquila allied with the Morellos to fight the Camorra. In 1917, both Morano and Vollero were convicted of murder and sentenced to life in prison. With their leadership gone, the two Camorra gangs disappeared and D'Aquila took over many of their rackets in Brooklyn. Soon after, Aquila also brought in the Mineo gang, making Mineo his first lieutenant. D'Aquila now controlled the largest and most influential Italian gang in New York City.

Prohibition

In 1920, the United States outlawed the production and sale of alcoholic beverages (Prohibition), creating the opportunity for an extremely lucrative illegal racket for the New York gangs. Around that time, two more Mafia gangs emerged in New York City. The first gang was a break-away faction from the Morello crime family based in the Bronx and led by Gaetano Reina, who had formerly been aligned with boss Ciro "The Artichoke King" Terranova. The second gang formed in the late 1920s in Brooklyn and was led by Joe Profaci.

By 1920, D'Aquila's only significant rival was Giuseppe "Joe the Boss" Masseria. Masseria had taken over the Morello family interests, and by the mid-1920, had begun to amass power and influence to rival that of D'Aquila. By the late 1920s, D'Aquila and Masseria were headed for a showdown.

On October 10, 1928 Masseria gunmen assassinated D'Aquila outside his home. D'Aquila's second-in-command, Alfred Mineo, and his top lieutenant, Steve Ferrigno, now commanded the largest and most influential Sicilian gang in New York City.

Castellammarese War

In 1930, the Castellammarese War started between
Masseria and Salvatore Maranzano, the new leader of Cola
Schirò's Castellammarese gang, for control of Italian-
American organized crime in New York. Mineo was a
casualty; he and Ferrigno were shot dead during an
assassination attempt on Masseria on November 5, 1930.

Lucky Luciano

On April 15, 1931, gangster Charles "Lucky" Luciano
invited his boss Giuseppe "Joe the Boss" Masseria to lunch
at Nuova Villa Tammaro in Coney Island, Brooklyn.
Masseria ate well that day, ordering veal, linguini, and red
wine, and after the meal he and his trusted lieutenant
whiled away the afternoon playing cards. It was a welcome
break for Masseria from the tensions of what would
become known as the Castellammarese War.

Salvatore Maranzano

On that spring day at the Coney Island restaurant, Masseria and Luciano played hand after hand. The usually suspicious Masseria relaxed and enjoyed himself. As the afternoon shadows grew longer along the boardwalk, Luciano put his cards face down on the table and excused himself. He had to go to the bathroom, he told his boss. Masseria watched him head toward the rear of the restaurant. As soon as Luciano was out of sight, four men came in through the front door—Albert Anastasia, Vito Genovese, Joe Adonis, and Bugsy Siegel. They each pulled out a gun and opened fire on the startled Masseria who took six shots and died on the spot. Luciano came out of the bathroom, looked down at the slain boss, and nodded approvingly to the hit team.

When word of Masseria's murder got out, Luciano brokered a truce with Salvatore Maranzano, who declared himself the Boss of Bosses.

The Castellammarese War was over.

But Maranzano's reign was short. A few months after Masseria's death, Luciano struck again. According to John H. Davis in his book Mafia Dynasty, four hired guns from the Lansky-Siegel gang wearing treasury agent uniforms went to Maranzano's office where the boss was expecting a surprise audit from the IRS. As Tommy Lucchese, who was in on the plot, kept Maranzano busy in the inner office, the killers disarmed his bodyguards in the waiting room. Two of the hit men held the guards at gunpoint while "the other two burst into Maranzano's office and shot and stabbed him to death."

With the dominant "Mustache Petes" now out of the way, New York was ready to realize Luciano's dream, a new national syndicate that would encourage cooperation among gangs regardless of ethnic origin. Lucky Luciano would bring the Mafia into the modern age, putting the group into organized crime. Out of the ruins of the Masseria and Maranzano gangs would emerge the Five Families of New York. One of the most powerful would become known as the Gambino Family.

In September 1931, Maranzano was himself assassinated in his office by a squad of contract killers. The main beneficiary (and organizer of both hits) was Charlie "Lucky" Luciano. Luciano kept Maranzano's five families and added a Commission to mediate disputes and prevent more gang warfare.

Also in 1931, Luciano replaced Scalise with Vincent Mangano as head of the D'Aquila/Mineo gang, now the Mangano crime family. Mangano also received a seat on the new Commission. The modern era of the Cosa Nostra had begun.

Mangano era

Vincent Mangano now took over the family, with his brother Philip as consigliere and Albert Anastasia as underboss. Vincent Mangano still believed in the Old World mob traditions of "honor", "tradition", "respect" and "dignity." However, he was somewhat more forward-looking than either Masseria or Maranzano. To compensate for loss of massive revenues with the end of Prohibition in 1933, Vincent Mangano moved his family into extortion, union racketeering, and illegal gambling operations including horse betting, running numbers and lotteries.

Vincent Mangano also established the City Democratic Club, ostensibly to promote American values. In reality, the Club was as a cover for Murder, Inc., the notorious band of mainly Jewish hitmen who performed contract murders for the Cosa Nostra nationwide. Anastasia was the operating head of Murder Inc.; he was popularly known as the "Lord High Executioner".

The Lord High Executioner

Vincent Mangano

After the murders of Masseria and Maranzano, one old-school Mafioso managed to survive the purge and thrive among the young Turks: Vincent Mangano. Though he was included in Lucky Luciano's plans to remodel organized crime in America, he still retained many of his old-world ways. He was tolerated because of his close association with Emil Camarda, vice-president of the International Longshoremen's Association, which gave Mangano tight control of rackets on the docks. Mangano and Camarda established the City Democratic Club, which promoted bedrock American values in the front room, while illegal activities were hatched in the backroom. It became a regular meeting place for the members of Murder, Inc., the infamous gang of assassins who were mostly Jewish and who, for a price, did the bidding of the Italian mobsters.

Mangano's cutthroat brother Philip frequented the club as did Albert Anastasia, the brutal, hot-headed mobster who was also knows at the "Mad Hatter," "Il Terremoto" (the Earthquake), and the "Lord High Executioner" of Murder, Inc. Of all the killers in that elite group, Anastasia was the most feared, and for good reason.

Vincent Mangano also had close ties with Emil Camarda, a vice-president of the International Longshoremen's Association (ILA). Through the ILA, Mangano and the family completely controlled the Manhattan and Brooklyn waterfronts. From 1932 onward, the president of ILA Local 1814 was Anthony "Tough Tony" Anastasio, Albert Anastasia's younger brother (Anthony kept the original spelling of their last name). Anastasio was one of the family's biggest earners, steering millions of dollars in kickbacks and payoffs into the family's coffers. Anastasio made no secret of his ties to the mob; he only had to say "my brother Albert" to get his point across. With the family's backing, the Brooklyn waterfront was Anastasio's bailiwick for 30 years.

Around this time, Carlo Gambino was promoted within the Mangano family, along with another future boss, Gambino's cousin Paul Castellano.

Anastasia and the Mangano brothers were usually in conflict, even though they worked together for 20 years. On numerous occasions, Anastasia and Vincent Mangano came close to physical conflict. Vincent Mangano felt uncomfortable with Anastasia's close ties to Luciano and other top mobsters outside his family. Mangano was also jealous of Anastasio's strong power base in Murder Inc. and the waterfront unions. In April 1951, Vincent Mangano disappeared without a trace, while his brother Philip was found dead. No one was ever charged in the Mangano brothers' deaths, and Vincent's body was never found. However, it is generally believed that Anastasia murdered both of them.

Anastasia regime

Called to face the Commission, Anastasia refused to accept guilt for the Mangano murders. However, Anastasia did claim that Vincent Mangano had been planning to kill him. Anastasia was already running the family in Vincent Mangano's "absence", and the Commission members were intimidated by Anastasia. With the support of Frank Costello, boss of the Luciano crime family, the Commission confirmed Anastasia's ascension as boss of what was now the Anastasia crime family. Carlo Gambino, a wily character with designs on the leadership himself, maneuvered himself into position as underboss.

The former boss of Murder Inc., Anastasia was a vicious murderer who inspired fear throughout the New York families. With Costello as an ally, Anastasia came to control the Commission. Costello's bitter rival was Vito Genovese, a former underboss for Luciano. Since 1946, Genovese had been scheming to remove Costello from power, but was not powerful enough to face Anastasia.

Albert Anastasia

Anastasia had been "close to some thirty assassinations with gun and ice pick and strangling rope, either in person or by direction," write Burton B. Turkus and Sid Feder in Murder, Inc. "The killings claimed by the torpedoes of the troop he commanded ran well into three figures." Though formally aligned with the Mangano family, Anastasia preferred the company of gangsters from other families, particularly Lucky Luciano, Frank Costello, and Louis Lepke, which didn't sit well with Vincent Mangano. Over the years, Anastasia's relationship with his boss deteriorated to the point where they nearly came to blows on several occasions and had to be physically separated.

Amazingly the two men coexisted within the same criminal organization for almost 20 years before the Lord High Executioner finally had enough. Anastasia's first move was against Vincent's vicious brother, Philip, who was shot symmetrically in each cheek and the back of the head. On April 19, 1951, Philip's body was found in the wetlands of Sheepshead Bay, Brooklyn, fully dressed except for his pants.

At about the same time, Vincent Mangano was reported missing. He was never found, and it was just assumed that he had met a fate similar to his brother's.

Attorney (l) with Albert Anastasia

It was assumed Anastasia was behind the rubout of the Mangano brothers, and he was called on the carpet by the other New York bosses. Anastasia never admitted to having any part of the murders, but he did tell the bosses that Vince Mangano had put out a contract on his head before he disappeared, which was confirmed by Anastasia's pal Frank Costello. Anastasia, who was already running the Mangano organization as his own, was too powerful—and too crazy—to be denied. The New York bosses formally agreed that he should be the new boss of the Mangano family.

Frank Costello

Anastasia now had control of a large portion of the Brooklyn waterfront. Besides having his family's "muscle" behind him, he was also one of the overseers of Murder Inc., the new national crime syndicate's lethal enforcement squad. Made up of seasoned killers from various ethnic gangs, Murder Inc.'s mandate was to carry out hits strictly for "business" reasons since making money was the syndicate's sole purpose. But with kill-crazy Anastasia at the helm, rival gangsters were usually careful not to offend him on any level.

Willie Moretti

Anastasia was such a powerful force that Frank Costello crossed family lines and formed an alliance with the Mad Hatter to provide protection. Costello, who was running the Luciano (later called the Genovese) Family while Lucky was in prison and later deported, was known as the Prime Minister of the Underworld for his unique ability to broker lucrative deals. He was an executive gangster who had initially depended on New Jersey mobster Willie Moretti to back him up with a force of over 50 loyal soldiers. But when an untreated syphilis infection began to take Moretti's mind, Vito Genovese, who was angling to take over the Luciano Family, proposed to the commission that Moretti be taken out of his misery before he inadvertently started revealing mob secrets. Three, possibly four, gunmen shot down Moretti on October 4, 1951, in a New Jersey restaurant. Without Moretti's services at his disposal, Costello turned to Anastasia and his troops to back him up. Anastasia, who had always liked Costello, obliged.

Anastasia's violent temper often got the better of him. While watching television one night in 1952, he saw an interview with a Brooklyn man named Arnold Schuster who described his experiences as a prosecution witness against famed bank robber Willie Sutton. Anastasia became enraged and shouted at the television set. "I can't stand squealers!" he yelled and immediately arranged for a hit team to kill Schuster. Oddly, Anastasia had no connection with Willie Sutton whatsoever. He just hated "squealers."

Albert Anatasia & wife

Schuster's murder was a serious violation of syndicate rules. Killing civilians was strictly off limits, and the ambitious Vito Genovese leapt on this breech, declaring to the Mafia commission that Anastasia was seriously unbalanced and thus a threat to the syndicate. He knew that if Anastasia could be eliminated, Costello would lose his muscle, and he would be free to take over the Luciano family. And if the commission refused his request, Genovese had another ace up his sleeve. Anastasia had no idea that his own underboss, the wily Carlo Gambino, had secretly sided with Genovese and brought crime boss Joe Profaci (of what would eventually become known as the Colombo Family) into the plot.

The pieces were in motion. On May 2, 1957, Costello walked into his apartment building on Central Park West. He didn't notice the black Cadillac pulling up to the curb outside. A 300-pound man lumbered out of the car, rushed into the lobby, and ducked behind a pillar as he pulled out a gun. "This is for you, Frank," he shouted. Costello turned toward the fat man as the gun went off. The bullet grazed Costello's scalp above the ear. The fat man ran back to the Cadillac, leaving the job unfinished. The wound was minor and Costello survived, but the incident got him to think about retirement. (The rotund shooter, who was never arrested, is reputed to be Vincent "Chin" Gigante who would lose weight and go on to become boss of the Genovese family in the late 1980s.)

Plot against Anastasia

Anastasia's own brutal actions soon created a favorable climate in New York for his removal. In 1952, Anastasia ordered the murder of a Brooklyn man Arnold Schuster who had aided in the capture of bank robber Willie Sutton. Anastasia did not like the fact that Schuster had helped the police. The New York families were outraged by this gratuitous killing that raised a large amount of public furor. Anastasia also alienated one of Luciano's powerful associates, Meyer Lansky by opening casinos in Cuba to compete with Lansky's. Genovese and Lansky soon recruited Carlo Gambino to the conspiracy by offering him the chance to replace Anastasia.

In May 1957, Costello escaped a Genovese-organized murder attempt with a minor injury and decided to resign as boss. However, Genovese and Gambino soon learned that Costello was conspiring with Anastasia to regain power. They decided to kill Anastasia.

On the morning of October 25, six months after the attempt on Costello's life, Albert Anastasia sat in a barber's chair in the Park Sheraton Hotel on Seventh Avenue, getting a trim. Two men in suits and fedoras with scarves covering their faces walked briskly into the barbershop, holding handguns down at their sides. One of them shoved Anastasia's barber out of the way, and they both started shooting. Anastasia took several bullets but managed to get to his feet, enraged that anyone would have the audacity to try to take out the Lord High Executioner. He lunged at his attackers, but in his confusion he actually lunged at their reflections in the large mirror that covered one wall. The killers then finished him off. Anastasia lay sprawled on the floor, his blood mingling with the fallen hair clippings. The identities of the two killers were never established, but it is known that they were members of the Profaci Family. Carlo Gambino had given the contract to Joe Profaci who passed the assignment along to "Crazy Joe" Gallo and his two brothers.

With Anastasia in the grave, the way was clear for the ascendance of the namesake of the Gambino Family, the real Godfather.

Gambino era

Carlo Gambino

Carlo Gambino was a diminutive man with small eyes and a large nose. Joseph Bonanno, who was the boss of his own family, characterized Gambino "a squirrel of a man." Unassuming in appearance, he hardly looked the part of a major-league crime boss, but in his case looks were indeed misleading. Though he eschewed ostentatious mansions, flashy cars, and sharp suits, he was perhaps the most intelligent and most powerful of any mob boss of any era. With the cunning of a fox and the stealthy bite of a viper, Carlo Gambino was in spirit a descendent of the cutthroat Borgias of the Renaissance.

Aniello Dellacroce

With Albert Anastasia out of the way, Gambino ascended
to the boss's chair and named Aniello Dellacroce, another
stone-cold killer who had been closely aligned to
Anastasia, as his underboss. With Dellacroce in a position
of power, Gambino was able to keep Anastasia's loyal
supporters in line.

Lucky Luciano

Gambino had the rare ability to see two moves ahead and act without hesitation when he saw an advantage. When it became evident to him that the ambitious Vito Genovese was not content with control of just his own family, Gambino laid a trap for him. Genovese, who longed to be Boss of All Bosses, knew that Frank Costello, Meyer Lansky, and Lucky Luciano were his enemies, but he never suspected that Gambino, who had helped him eliminate Anastasia, was secretly in league with the others. Many of the Mafia bosses staunchly opposed getting into the narcotics trade, but Genovese saw the huge profits that could be reaped from drug dealing, and he allowed it in his family. His enemies recognized an opportunity. They put together a lucrative drug deal that was too good for Genovese to pass up, and then paid a Puerto Rican drug dealer $100,000 to rat on Genovese

. The government chose to ignore the fact that in all probability a small-fish drug pusher wouldn't have had access to a big-fish Mafia boss and that whatever testimony he gave would be hearsay, but they wanted Genovese so badly, they took the little fish's testimony as gospel truth and won a conviction against Genovese that earned him a 15-year sentence.

Gambino quickly built the family into the most powerful crime family in the United States. He was helped by Meyer Lansky's offshore gaming houses in Cuba and the Bahamas, a lucrative business for the Cosa Nostra.

Control of other crime families

Vito Genovese

Despite all the treachery and double-dealing Gambino used to seize power, he also knew when to make peace and forge alliances. In 1962 his son Thomas married Frances Lucchese, daughter of Tommy "Three-Finger Brown" Lucchese, who was the boss of the powerful New York family that bore his name. Like a Machiavellian prince, Gambino gave the young couple his blessing as he anticipated the benefits he would gain from a familial bond between two major crime families.

Tommy "Three Fingers" Lucchese

Under Gambino's leadership, family rackets spread into new areas. Starting in the late '50s, they engaged in large-scale drug trafficking. The Gambino and Lucchese families put a stranglehold on illegal activities at JFK International Airport, effectively boxing out all competition. Gambino bought into all kinds of legitimate businesses such as pizza parlors, meat markets, and restaurants, construction companies, trucking firms, dress factories, and nightclubs, and used them as fronts to facilitate illegal operations.

In 1964, Joseph "Joe Bananas" Bonanno, the head of the Bonanno crime family and Joseph Magliocco, the new boss of the Profaci crime family, conspired to kill Gambino and his allies on the Commission. However, the man entrusted with the job, Joseph Colombo, instead revealed the plot to Gambino. Led by Gambino, the Commission forced Magliocco to resign and hand over his family to Colombo, while Bonanno fled New York. Gambino had now become the most powerful leader of the "Five Families".

In 1967, when an ailing Tommy Lucchese stepped aside and appointed Carmine Tramunti to take over as boss of his family, Gambino supported the new boss who was really no more than a figurehead and once again pulled the strings from behind the curtain. As the war in Vietnam was raging and student protesters rioted on campuses across America, Carlo Gambino had firm and comfortable hold in his own family and considerable influence over two other families.

As Joseph Coffey and Jerry Schmetterer write in *The Coffey Files: One Cop's War Against the Mob*, "the general opinion of Castellano was the he was selfish, greedy, and not as smart as he liked people to believe. Dellacroce," they argued, "was the real brains of the family." But Dellacroce was a traditionalist, and he wouldn't challenge a boss's decision. Dellacroce's supporters simmered, unhappy with Gambino's choice.

Anthony Scotto (l) with Attorney La Rosa

Gambino increased his family's presence in the Teamsters Union, in Manhattan's garment center, and in the trash disposal business in all five boroughs. He solidified the family's control of the Brooklyn waterfront when one of his capos, Anthony Scotto, rose to power in the AFL-CIO International Longshoreman's Association, which in the late '70s had 100,000 members working ports from Maine to Texas. Scotto also became president of the union's Local 1814 in Brooklyn. Many people found it hard to believe that the well-spoken, college-educated Scotto was a member of the Mafia, and his close ties with elected officials helped him maintain his respectable image. He raised money for New York Gov. Hugh L. Carey's reelection bid in 1978 and for Lt. Gov. Mario Cuomo's unsuccessful run for mayor of New York City in 1977. When Scotto was brought to trial for taking cash payoffs from waterfront businesses, no less than Gov. Carey and two former New York mayors, John Lindsay and Robert Wagner, testified on his behalf. Scotto was ultimately convicted, but the judge imposed a light sentence after receiving pleas for leniency from a number of prominent people in labor, business, and politics.

Joe Colombo

Carlo Gambino also had a gift for making lemonade out of
bitter lemons. In the early '60s, Joe Bonanno and Joe
Mogliocco, the newly appointed boss of the Profaci Family,
felt that they were being pushed around by the more
powerful bosses, so they hatched a plot to level the
underworld playing field by secretly putting out contracts
on the lives of Gambino and Tommy Lucchese as well as
the bosses of Buffalo and Los Angeles. The contract was
given to Profaci Family hitman Joe Colombo, who
suddenly saw an opportunity to better his own situation.
Colombo informed the intended victims of the plot, and
they in turn went to the Mafia commission for justice. The
commission ruled that the elderly Mogliocco could live if
he retired. Bonanno defied the commission and as a result
was kidnapped and held captive until he agreed to give up
complete control of his family and retire to Arizona.

The commission rewarded hitman Colombo with Mogliocco's former position as head of the family that would eventually take Colombo's name. But Colombo was widely regarded as unfit for the job and overly dependent on Gambino's advice.

In 1971, Gambino allegedly used his power to orchestrate the shooting of Colombo. Gambino and his allies were unhappy about Colombo's high public profile. On June 28, 1971; Jerome Johnson shot Colombo at a Manhattan rally. Johnson was tentatively linked to the Gambino family, but no one else was charged in the shooting. Colombo survived the shooting, but remained paralyzed until his death in 1978.

Gambino's influence also stretched into behind-the-scenes control of the Lucchese crime family, led by Carmine "Mr. Gribbs" Tramunti.

In 1972, Gambino allegedly picked Frank "Funzi" Tieri to be front boss of the Genovese crime family. Gambino had allegedly ordered the murder of Tieri's predecessor, Thomas Eboli, after Eboli failed to repay a $3 million loan to Gambino. It is also more likely believed Eboli was killed by own crime family for his erratic ways.

Under Gambino, the family gained particularly strong influence in the construction industry. It acquired behind-the-scenes control of Teamsters Local 282, which controlled access to most building materials in the New York area and could literally bring most construction jobs in New York City to a halt.

Gambino's health began to fail in the 1970s, and as time passed, he was seen in public less and less.

He nevertheless maintained tight control over his family, running his rackets from his retreat in Massapequa, Long Island. In his final years he anointed his own successor, his cousin and brother-in-law Paul Castellano, which angered the traditionalists in the family who felt that underboss Aniello Dellacroce was the obvious choice.

On October 15, 1976, Gambino died of a heart attack. Following Gambino's wishes, control of the family passed to Paul Castellano, whose sister was married to Gambino. Castellano kept longtime underboss Aniello Dellacroce in his position. Many Dellacroce allies were bitterly disappointed by Castellano's ascension, but Dellacroce insisted that they obey Gambino's instructions.

John Gotti in cuffs, 1974

A man who was staunchly loyal to Dellacroce was part of an incident in 1972 that would have major repercussions years later. Carlo Gambino's nephew, Manny Gambino, was kidnapped and held for a $350,000 ransom, which the boss paid in part. The kidnappers reneged on the deal and killed Manny, burying his body in a New Jersey landfill. The boss wanted revenge, and the family assembled a list of likely suspects, one of them was James McBratney, who had a history of kidnapping wiseguys for profit. In truth, McBratney had nothing to do with the incident. Nevertheless three Gambino soldiers cornered him in a Staten Island bar and killed him for the crime. One of the three executioners was John Gotti, who was convicted for the crime. Upon his release from prison he was made a capo for his good deed. Gotti would go on to become one of Dellacroce's most powerful supporters, and after

Dellacroce's death, he would become boss of the family.
But not before the reign of "Big Paul" Castellano.

Castellano regime

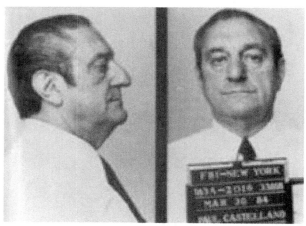

Paul Castellano

When Castellano became boss, he negotiated a division of responsibilities between himself and Dellacroce. Castellano took control of the so-called "white collar" crimes that included stock embezzlement and other big money rackets. Dellacroce retained control of the traditional Cosa Nostra activities. To maintain control over the Dellacroce faction, Castellano relied on the crew run by Anthony "Nino" Gaggi and Roy DeMeo. The DeMeo crew allegedly committed from 74 to 200 murders during the late 1970s and mid-1980s.

During his regime, Castellano vastly expanded the family's influence in the construction industry. His new alliance with the Irish-American Westside Gang made millions of dollars for the family in construction rackets. For all intents and purposes, the Gambinos held veto power over all construction projects worth over $2 million in New York City. The DeMeo gang also ran a very lucrative car theft ring. Castellano relied on a four-man ruling panel to supervise family operations. This panel consisted of powerful Garment District leader Thomas Gambino, bodyguard and later underboss Thomas Bilotti, and powerful Queens faction-leaders Daniel Marino and James Failla.

Manhattan vs. Brooklyn

As clever and foresighted as Carlo Gambino was, he left his family divided and embittered when he died. The Gambinos had split into two camps: the Manhattan faction, who was loyal to Dellacroce, and the Brooklyn faction which sided with the new boss, Paul Castellano. "Big Paul" had thrown a bone to the Manhattan faction by keeping Dellacroce on as his underboss, but it wasn't enough to stop the backroom grumbling. The Manhattan faction believed that Castellano wasn't half the gangster that Dellacroce was and that Castellano had simply inherited the position instead of earning it.

Carlo Gambino

The two factions had different philosophies regarding organized crime. The Dellacroce faction valued traditional mob rackets—gambling, street-level extortion, narcotics trafficking, prostitution, loan sharking, and hijacking—the so-called "blue collar crimes," while the Castellano faction favored "white collar crimes" such as high-level extortion, bribery, and theft in labor, construction, waste management, the garment industry, on the docks, and at JKF Airport. Castellano wanted to further Carlo Gambino's master plan of using ill-gotten gains to buy into legitimate businesses, but eventually the Manhattan faction began to feel that their profits were being funneled to a boss who wanted everything to be legit and cared little for the workhorse crews who did the dirty work. They feared that if all family operations eventually became legit, there would be no place for the hard-core criminals who took their cues from Dellacroce and revered the memory of Albert Anastasia.

Although Castellano adopted an executive style, he maintained a significant contingent of tough guys in his faction to keep Dellacroce's Manhattan faction in check. One of the premier crews in the Manhattan faction was Carmine "Wagon Wheels" Fatico's, which included an up-and-coming John Gotti. Fatico's crew was into bookmaking, loan-sharking, gambling, and hijacking, particularly at JFK Airport, and they had a reputation for using violence to get what they wanted when they wanted it. But the Brooklyn faction had a crew that was even more violent, some were certifiable psychopaths, led by capo Roy DeMeo. Working out of the Flatlands section of Brooklyn, DeMeo, who was a trained butcher by trade, had taught his young protégés how to kill cleanly and efficiently. As described by Gene Mustain and Jerry Capeci in *Murder Machine*, this crew specialized in draining the blood from bodies, cutting them up into small pieces, wrapping the pieces into small packages, and disposing of them so they wouldn't be found. The apartment at the rear of their regular hangout, the Gemini Lounge, was occupied by one of DeMeo's cousins, Joseph "Dracula" Guglielmo, and dozens of people were known to have met their end in that apartment.

If anyone in the Manhattan faction entertained thoughts of challenging Paul Castellano, the idea of tangling with DeMeo's demented crew gave them pause—at least until DeMeo was found dead in the trunk of his Cadillac in 1983. He'd been shot five times behind both ears.

The rank and file's dissatisfaction with Castellano grew as the years passed. They resented his aloofness and apparent disdain for the foot soldiers in his family as exemplified by his remote mansion, which he called the "White House," in the Todt Hill section of Staten Island, the highest point in the five boroughs. They became outraged when rumors spread that the boss had been having an affair with Gloria Orlate, his Colombian maid, while his wife was still living in the house. These rumors were confirmed by FBI tapes obtained from a bug planted in a lamp on his kitchen table. The feds caught Big Paul discussing illegal deals with his underlings and whispering sweet nothings to Olarte. According to Joseph F. O'Brien and Andrew Kurins, two of the agents who planted the bug, in their book *Boss of Bosses: The Fall of the Godfather— The FBI and Paul Castellano*, the boss "doted on her... Like adolescents... the pair indulged in long sessions of kissing and petting, stroking and teasing without ever having actual intercourse." Castellano would later undergo surgery to regain his sexual prowess for her. To the men of honor in the Gambino family, this was no way for a boss to act.

It seemed that everything Castellano did rubbed the Manhattan faction the wrong way. He made a pact with Genovese family boss Vincent "Chin" Gigante to execute, without warning or appeal, any member caught dealing drugs. Many wiseguys in the Gambino family were heavily into the drug trade and depended on those profits, including several members of Carmine Fatico's crew.

By the early 1980s, Castellano faced RICO charges in two upcoming trials—the Commission case which sought to put away the heads of the five New York families and a case that targeted Roy DeMeo's stolen luxury car ring. Castellano decided to plan ahead in case he was convicted and had to serve time. He let it be known that Thomas Gambino, Carlo's son, would take over for him and Tommy Bilotti would serve as underboss. The Manhattan faction seethed. They considered Thomas Gambino even more white collar than Castellano and had little respect for Bilotti who, though a capo, served as Castellano's chauffeur and bodyguard.

Gambino family case

In response to the Gambino rise, federal prosecutors targeted the family leadership. On March 31, 1984 a federal grand jury indicted Castellano and 20 other Gambino members and associates with charges of drug trafficking, murder, theft, and prostitution. This group included John Gotti's brother, Gene, and his best friend, Angelo Ruggiero. In early 1985, Castellano was indicted along with other Cosa Nostra leaders in the Mafia Commission case. Facing the possibility of time in prison, Castellano announced that Thomas Gambino would become acting boss in Castellano's absence, with Bilotti as acting underboss to replace the ailing Dellacrocce.

Although the Gambino family was making more money, the internal strife continued to grow. The Dellacroce faction considered Castellano a businessman, not a mob boss. They grew infuriated when Castellano increased their tribute requirements while building himself a grand mansion in Staten Island. Castellano became increasingly detached from family members, conducting all family business at his mansion. Castellano's announcement about Gambino and Bilotti further enraged the Dellacroce partisans.

Conflict with Gotti

In 1983, a federal indictment charged 13 members of the Gambino family with drug trafficking. This group included John Gotti's brother, Gene, and his best friend, Angelo "Quack Quack" Ruggiero, who got his nickname for his nonstop talking. Unbeknownst to him, the feds had been listening in on his home phone conversations since 1980, and they had the chatty Ruggiero on tape discussing family business, making drug deals, and expressing contempt for Castellano, calling him a "pansy" and a "milk drinker" among other things. By law, when a person is charged with a crime based on evidence gathered from a wiretap, he's given transcripts of the taped material to aid in his defense. Ruggiero was presented with boxes of such transcripts, and it wasn't long before Big Paul sent down word that he wanted to see them. If his men were dealing dope, he wanted to know about it. Ruggiero told Castellano that he was innocent, that it was a bum rap, and that the feds had no case against him. (In fact, Ruggiero had borrowed $200,000 from Castellano for a drug deal, telling the boss that it was for a pornography enterprise.) Castellano, however, could not be placated. He insisted that he see the transcripts.

Ruggiero went to underboss Aniello Dellacroce for help. Dellacroce managed to stall Castellano through 1984 and into 1985, but Castellano persisted. He wanted a copy of Ruggiero's transcripts, and as his own trials drew near, he felt that it was crucial to know what had been going on in his family behind his back. By now the 70-year-old Dellacroce was dying of cancer and couldn't be of much help to Ruggiero, but Ruggiero's childhood friend, John Gotti, rallied to his side. The white-collar boss from up on the hill was not going to interfere with the business of the real wiseguys. Castellano was losing his patience with these insolent soldiers. He informed his inner circle that if he didn't get the transcripts soon, he would have Ruggiero and Gotti whacked. Rumors of his intentions filtered through the ranks and found their way to Gotti.

On December 2, 1985, Dellacroce died of cancer. With Dellacrocce gone, Ruggiero could no longer keep the incriminating transcripts away from Castellano. Gotti quickly realized that now was the best time to murder Castellano and seize power. But Castellano was at risk, too. If he attempted to take out Ruggiero and Gotti, the Manhattan faction was ready to go to war against the rest of the family, threatening to destroy what had become the dominant criminal organization in New York City. Each day the tensions mounted. For John Gotti and his crew, the choice soon became evident: Kill or be killed. If there was ever any doubt in John Gotti's mind, it was Paul Castellano himself who provided the last straw. Big Paul did not attend Aniello Dellacroce's wake. To the Manhattan faction, this was an unforgivable show of disrespect

On December 16, just after 5 p.m., the streets of midtown Manhattan were jammed with office workers and Christmas shoppers. Rush hour had begun, worse than usual during the holiday season, and a black Lincoln Continental inched along with the crush of traffic. Bilotti and Castellano arrived at the Sparks Steak House in Manhattan for a dinner meeting with capo Frank DeCicco. Eight hit men waited for their arrival. The primary team of four wore identical trench coats and fur Cossack hats and lingered in the doorways along the block where the steakhouse was located. The backup team hung back nearby in case they were needed. Castellano's car arrived at about 5:30 p.m. As the boss opened his door to get out, the hit team converged. Castellano and Bilotti took six bullets each, the hubbub of rush-hour traffic masking the sound of the shots. The sight of two men in business suits sprawled on the pavement alerted pedestrians that something had happened. Bilotti's body was face up in the middle of East 46th Street, blocking traffic. Big Paul had toppled into the gutter and lay in a contorted position with blood pooling around him. As people gathered around, the assassins walked quickly to waiting cars. Eye witnesses said they saw the identically dressed men but were unable to identify any of them individually.

Big Paul had toppled into the gutter and lay in a contorted
position with blood pooling around him

Bilotti's body was face up in the middle of East 46th Street

In a matter of weeks the newspapers declared John Gotti,
the man who had organized the hit, as the new boss of the

Gambino family. In one bold move, he deposed an unpopular leader, averted a mob civil war, and saved his own hide. The ascent of John Gotti would mark a return to the methods of Gotti's idol, Albert Anastasia, the Lord High Executioner.

The Last Don

John Gotti, 1987

John Gotti is perhaps the most well-known Mafioso in American history, on par with the legendary Al Capone. He had a violent temper and was quick to retaliate against the smallest perceived slight, and yet like Capone, he was a stylish man about town, known for his hand-tailored suits, painted silk ties, and perfectly coifed steel gray hair. While most mob bosses shunned the media, Gotti always had a quip ready for the outstretched microphones and a million-dollar smile for the cameras whenever he strutted into court. The press dubbed him the Dapper Don for his sartorial style, then the Teflon Don for his astounding ability to keep criminal charges from sticking to him. He had the bark of a pit bull and the bite of a Great White, but the New York public took to him and despite his reputation, seemed to root for him whenever he was on trial.

Gotti regime

Right after the Castellano murder, John Gotti was chosen as the new boss of the Gambino crime family. Gotti appointed DeCicco as underboss and promoted Ruggiero to Caporegime. While maintaining his old hangout, the Bergin Hunt and Fish Club in Ozone Park, Queens, he mainly held court at the Aniello Dellacroce's old haunt, the Ravenite Club on Mulberry Street in Manhattan's Little Italy where he popularized the "walk-talk," conducting confidential conversations while strolling along the streets as news and surveillance cameras caught the video but not the audio. Unlike his contemporaries, Gotti loved the limelight, and a week didn't go by that a Gotti sighting wasn't reported somewhere in the press. At that time, future underboss Salvatore "Sammy the Bull" Gravano was allegedly elevated to Caporegime. Known as the "Dapper Don", Gotti was well known for his hand-tailored suits and silk ties. Unlike his colleagues, Gotti made little effort to hide his mob connections and was very willing to provide interesting sound bites to the media. Gotti's home in Howard Beach, Queens, was frequently seen on television. Gotti liked to hold meetings with family members while walking in public places so that law enforcement agents could not record the conversations. One of Gotti's neighbors in Howard Beach was his dear friend Joseph Massino, underboss of the Bonanno crime family.

Mob leaders from the other families were enraged at the Castellano murder and disapproved of Gotti's high-profile style. Gotti's strongest enemy was Genovese crime family boss Vincent "The Chin" Gigante, a former Castellano ally. Gigante conspired with Lucchese crime family leaders

Vittorio "Vic" Amuso and Anthony "Gaspipe" Casso, to put out a murder contract on Gotti's life.

Frank DeCicco

On April 13, 1986, Frank DeCicco--Gotti's underboss and the man who had set up Castellano—stood outside his parked Buick with a friend from the Lucchese family, Frank Bellino. As DeCicco reached into the car to fetch a business card for Bellino, a bomb concealed under the car exploded. DeCicco was nearly torn in half by the blast. Police arrived and rushed him to the hospital, but he was dead before he got there. Bellino was seriously injured but survived. The bomb was meant for John Gotti.

DeCicco's replacement, Joseph Armone, would be convicted of racketeering in 1987 alongside the family's consigliere Joseph N. Gallo.

Gotti seemed larger than life, untouchable and unstoppable. The government brought him to trial three times, and he beat the charges every time. But his luck fed his arrogance. He demanded that his men treat him like the Pope, bowing and scraping in his presence. When he called for them, he wanted them to appear instantly. Failing to show up could earn the offender a death sentence. "You know why he's dying?" Gotti was heard saying on an FBI wiretap on December 12, 1989, in reference to a wiseguy whose murder he had ordered. "He's gonna die because he refused to come in when I called. He didn't do nothing else wrong." Oddly, Gotti preferred to have his men by his side while he held court when they could have been out earning money for the family.

John Gotti

Gotti was tried three times by federal and state officials, but was acquitted each time, earning him the nickname "The Teflon Don." It turned out that the trials had been compromised by witness intimidation, juror misconduct and jury tampering. Gotti's flamboyance, however, proved to be his undoing. The FBI had managed to bug an apartment above the Ravenite Social Club in Little Italy, where an elderly widow let mobsters hold top-level meetings. Gotti was heard planning criminal activities and complaining about his underlings. In particular, he complained about Gravano, portraying him as a "mad dog" killer. The feds had allowed Gravano to hear the portions of the tapes where Gotti disparaged him, and Gravano decided to do the unthinkable: rat on the boss.Gravano responded by turning state's evidence and testifying against Gotti and other members of the family.

Sammy "The Bull" Gravano testifies

The tension in the courtroom was electric when Gravano testified against Gotti and his co-defendant, consigliere Frank Locascio. Gotti stared daggers at Gravano, but the Bull was undeterred as he recounted crime after crime that Gotti had either committed himself or ordered. On April 2, 1992, Gotti was convicted and received a sentence of life without parole. Gravano, who confessed to 19 murders committed between 1970 and 1990, was given five years. It was a sad day for the Gambino family, but as Carl Sifakis writes in *The Mafia Encyclopedia*, mobsters "privately acknowledged the Bull's charge that Gotti's arrogance had done much to bring down the boss and their organization."

The family since Gotti

Gotti continued to rule the family from prison, conveying messages through his brothers and son, John Jr. who visited him often. At the federal maximum-security penitentiary in Marion, Ill., Gotti was confined to a small cell by himself 23 hours a day. While he appealed his conviction, the day-to-day operation of the family shifted to capos John "Jackie Nose" D'Amico and Nicholas "Little Nick" Corozzo who agreed to take over as acting boss at the urging of Gotti's younger brother, Gene, when older brother, Peter, refused the position. But as Corozzo was getting ready to assume power, he was arrested on the beach in Key Biscayne, Fla., and two days before Christmas 1996. He pleaded guilty to racketeering charges and was sentenced to eight years in prison. Gotti's son took over as head of the family, but Junior, despite his imposing body-builder physique, lacked his father's toughness and criminal skills. In 1998, he too was convicted on racketeering charges and sentenced to 77 months in prison.

On June 10, 2002, John Gotti, the Teflon Don, died of throat and mouth cancer at a prison hospital in Springfield, Mo. He was 61 years old. When Gotti, Sr. died, his brother Peter took over as boss, allegedly alongside D'Amico, but the family's fortunes have dwindled to a remarkable extent given their power a few short decades ago, when they were considered the most powerful criminal organization on earth. By this time the Gambino Family was in disarray with membership down to around 150 from a high of 250, according to Carl Sifakis in *The Mafia Encyclopedia*. On July 15, 1999, journalist Jerry Capeci reported in his online Gangland column that only 5 of the 21 Gambino capos active in 1991 were still in business. Thirteen of them had been sentenced to prison, including Gotti's brother, Gene, and Carlo Gambino's son, Thomas. Collectively they had been forced to pay over $10 million in fines.

Peter Gotti was imprisoned as well in 2003, as the leadership allegedly went to the current administration members, Nicholas Corozzo, Jackie D'Amico and Joseph Corozzo.

As former rivals of John Gotti took completely over the Gambino family, mostly because the rest of Gotti's loyalists were either jailed or under indictments, and because Gotti, Sr died in prison in 2002, then-current head of white collar crimes and Caporegime, Michael "Mikey Scars" DiLeonardo turned state's evidence, due to increased law enforcement and credible evidence to be presented in his racketeering trial, and chose to testify against mobsters from all of the Five Families. One of the last Gotti supporters, DiLeonardo testified against, among others, Peter Gotti and Anthony "Sonny" Ciccone from 2003 to 2005, and disappeared into the Witness Protection Program. At the same time, Sammy Gravano, Gotti's former Underboss, had evaded the program in 1995 and was arrested and jailed for operating an Ecstasy-ring that stretched from Arizona to New York City in 2003. He's currently facing charges in New Jersey for the 1980 murder of a corrupt New York City policeman. During that same year, he was sentenced to 19 years in prison, ironically due to informants amongst his associates.

In 2005, Nicholas Corozzo and his longtime underling Leonard "Lenny" DiMaria were released from prison after serving ten years for racketeering and loansharking charges in New York and Florida. That same year, US law enforcement recognized Corozzo as the Boss of the Gambino crime family, with his brother Joseph Corozzo as the family Consigliere, Arnold "Zeke" Squitieri as the acting Underboss and Jackie D'Amico as a highly regarded member with the Corozzo brothers.

Jack Falcone

In 2002, then FBI agent Joaquin García infiltrated the
Gambino crime family under the alias of Jack Falcone.
Gambino capo Greg DePalma was so impressed by Falcone
that he offered to make him a family soldier. In 2005, the
FBI terminated Garcia's assignment out of fear that the
Gambinos might discover his true identity. However,
evidence gathered by Garcia allowed the government to
convict DePalma and several other Gambino leaders on
racketeering charges. DePalma was sentenced to twelve
years in federal prison.

Operation Old Bridge

Main article: Operation Old Bridge

On Thursday, February 7, 2008, an indictment was issued,
leading to the arrest of 54 people affiliated with the
Gambino family in New York City, its suburbs, New Jersey
and Long Island. This was the culmination of a four-year
FBI investigation known as Operation Old Bridge. A
federal grand jury later that day accused 62 people of
having ties to the Gambino crime family, and offenses such
as murders, conspiracy, drug trafficking, robberies,
extortion and other crimes were included in the indictment.
By the end of the week, more than 80 people were indicted
in the Eastern District of New York. The case is now
referred to as *United States of America v. Agate et al.* It was
assigned to Judge Nicholas Garaufis. The FBI used
informant Joseph Vollaro, the owner of a truck company on
Staten Island, who secretly recorded conversations between
himself and members of the Gambino family over the
previous three years.

Among the arrested were the current Gambino crime family leaders John "Jackie Nose" D'Amico, Joseph "Jo Jo" Corozzo and Domenico "Italian Dom" Cefalu, including Gambino family Caporegime Leonard "Lenny" DiMaria, Francesco "Frank" Cali, Thomas "Tommy Sneakers" Cacciopoli. However, recognized captain and co-acting boss Nicholas "Little Nick" Corozzo, one of the main leaders indicted in the case, fled his home on Long Island, acting on prior knowledge, and was considered a fugitive by US law enforcement, until his arrest before turning himself in on May 29, 2008, after almost four months on the run.

The federal operation broke up a growing alliance between the Gambinos and the Sicilian Mafia, which wanted to get further into the drug trade. One of those arrested in the raids in the US was Frank Cali, a captain in the Gambino family. He is allegedly the "ambassador" in the US for the Inzerillo crime family.

Current position

and leadership

From 2005 to 2008, federal authorities successfully prosecuted the Gambino administration, several capos, and many soldiers and associates. Since both federal and New York State authorities rounded up the entire Gambino family hierarchy in early 2008, a three-man panel of street bosses Daniel "Danny" Marino, John Gambino and Bartolomeo Vernace was running the Gambino family while the administration members were in prison. Marino, Vernace, Gambino, Cefalu, D'Amico, Nicholas Corozzo, and Arnold Squitieri have all been listed as leaders in the family. In July 2011, it was reported that Domenico Cefalu has been promoted to official boss of the crime family, putting an end to the Gotti regime. The current family is believed to have between 150 and 200 members as well as over 1500 associates.

Today the Gambino family still controls the piers in Brooklyn and Staten Island through infiltrated labor unions. A pair of indictments in 2009 and 2010, respectively, shows that the family is still very active in New York City. During 2009, the Gambino family saw many important members released from prison. In 2009, former National Basketball Association (NBA) referee Tim Donaghy accused Gambino associate James Battista of using Donaghy's knowledge of NBA games to pick winners in illegal sports gambling. On November 18, 2009, the NYPD arrested 22 members and associates of the Lucchese and Gambino crime families as part of "Operation Pure Luck". The raid was a result of cases involving loan sharking and sports gambling on Staten Island. There were also charges of bribing New York City court officers and Sanitation Department officials.

The glory days of the Gambino Family are over. Carlo Gambino's successors did not learn his lessons well enough to keep their mouths shut, maintain a low profile, and prosper from the shadows. The family's diminished power and influence can be seen today in John Gotti's two main hangouts. The Bergin Hunt and Fish Club where Gotti ran his crew and hatched the plot to murder Paul Castellano has been subdivided. The wiseguys now share the space with a butcher's shop and delicatessen. The Ravenite Club in Little Italy, which was the court of the Mafia king, is now a ladies boutique run by a designer from Hong Kong.

Historical leadership of the Gambino crime family

Boss (official and acting)

1910–1928— Salvatore "Toto" D'Aquila – took over the Brooklyn Camorra in 1916 and merged with *"Al Mineo's gang"* forming the largest family in New York. He was killed on orders of boss Joe Masseria in 1928.

1928–1930—Alfred "Al Mineo" Manfredi – killed in Castellammarese War 1930.

1930–1931 — Francesco "Frank/Don Cheech" Scalise – demoted after murder of boss of all bosses Salvatore Maranzano.

1931–1951 — Vincenzo "Vincent" Mangano – disappeared in April 1951, allegedly killed on orders of underboss Albert Anastasia.

1951–1957 — Albert "Mad Hatter" Anastasia – murdered in October 1957 on orders of underboss Carlo Gambino.

1957–1976 — Carlo "The Godfather" Gambino – died of natural causes 1976.

Acting 1974–1976 — Paul Castellano – acting boss during Gambino's illness, became official boss after his death.

1976–1985 — Paul "Big Paul" Castellano – killed on orders of capo John Gotti.

1985–2002 — John "Dapper Don" Gotti – imprisoned in 1990, died in 2002.

Acting 1992–1999 — John A. Gotti, also known as John "Junior" Gotti, – imprisoned in 1999.

Acting 1999–2002 — Peter Gotti – promoted to official boss.

2002–2011 — Peter "One Eye" Gotti – imprisoned in 2002, serving life sentence.

Acting 2002–2005 — Arnold "Zeke" Squitieri

Acting 2005–2008 — Nicholas "Little Nick" Corozzo – convicted in 2008, projected release date is in 2020.

Acting 2008–2010 — **Ruling Committee/Panel**: Daniel Marino (jailed), Bartolomeo "Bobby" Vernace (jailed), and John Gambino.

2011–present – Domenico Cefalu

Street boss

Street boss is a position created 2005. It was the second most powerful position in the organization.

2005–2011 John "Jackie the Nose" D'Amico

Underboss

(Official and acting)

The underboss was traditionally the second most powerful position in the Gambino family (after the boss). However, the 2005 appointment of Jackie D'Amico as "street boss" made that position more important than underboss.

19??-1928 Alfred Mineo (his group merged with the *D'Aquila family* at the start of Prohibition. Mineo was killed in 1930)

1928–1930 Steve Ferrigno (killed in 1930)

1931–1951 Albert "Mad Hatter" Anastasia (became official boss in 1951)

1951–1957 Frank Scalice (murdered in 1957)

1957 Carlo Gambino (became official boss in 1957)

1957–1965 Joseph Biondo (removed by boss Carlo Gambino in 1965)

1965–1985 Aniello "Neil" Dellacroce (died of natural causes in 1985)

Acting 1974–1975 James "Jimmy Brown" Failla (replaced by Dellacroce after release from prison)

Dec 1985 Thomas Bilotti (Murdered in 1985 on orders of capo John Gotti after 11 days)

1985–1986 Frank DeCicco (murdered in 1986 by Lucchese crime family hitmen)

1986–1990 Joseph "Piney" Armone (imprisoned in 1986, died in prison 1992)

Acting 1986–1990 Frank Locascio (moved to acting consigliere in 1990)

1990–1991 Salvatore "Sammy the Bull" Gravano (turned government witness in 1991)

1991–1999 *Vacant*

1999–2012 Arnold "Squiggy" Squitieri

Acting 2002–2005 Anthony "The Genius" Megale (projected release date is December 1, 2014)

Acting 2005–2011 Domenico "Italian Dom" Cefalu (became boss)

2012–present Frank Cali

Consigliere

(Official and acting)

In Italian, consigliere means "advisor." The Consigliore's highest priority is to help the boss make decisions. Together, the boss, street boss, underboss, and consigliere are referred to as "the administration."

19??-1930 Giuseppe Triana

1931–1951 Philip Mangano

1951–1957 Giuseppe "Joe Bandy" Biondo

1957–1967 Joseph "Staten Island Joe" Riccobono

1967–1987 Joseph "Joe N." Gallo

1987–1990 Salvatore "Sammy the Bull" Gravano

1990–1992 Joseph "Joe Piney" Armone

1990–1992 Frank "Frankie Loc" Locascio

1992–1999

1999–present Joseph "Jo Jo" Corozzo (jailed since 2008, release date is January 5, 2015.)

Committee

Several capo committees have periodically replaced the underboss and consigliere positions, allowing an imprisoned boss better control of the family.

1991–1992 – *committee* John Gotti, Jr., James "Jimmy Brown" Failla, Nicholas "Little Nick" Corozzo, John "Jackie Nose" D'Amico, Louis "Big Lou" Vallario, Peter "Petey Boy" Gotti

1992–1993 – *committee* John "Junior" Gotti, James Failla, John D'Amico, Louis Vallario, Peter Gotti

1993–1994 – *committee* John "Junior" Gotti, Nicholas Corozzo, John D'Amico, Louis Vallario, Peter Gotti

1994–1996 – *committee* Nicholas Corozzo, John D'Amico, Louis Vallario, Peter Gotti

1996–1999 – *committee* John D'Amico, Louis Vallario, Peter Gotti

Administration

Boss Domenico Cefalu – A Sicilian-born mobster who started out as a heroin trafficker in the Family's Sicilian "Zip" faction. He was inducted into the organization in 1990 by John Gotti and joined the Pasquale Conte crew, a group that included relatives of Cefalu and held strong ties to Sicily. After being identified as acting underboss in the mid-2000s, Cefalu was eventually confirmed as the new boss of the family in 2011.

Underboss Frank Cali - Like Cefalu, Cali has strong ties to Sicily, in particular those close to his relative, John Gambino. Though he maintains association with the Sicilian faction, Cali was born and raised in New York City and eventually rose in stature within the regime of Jackie D'Amico. Cali was later identified as acting captain of this crew, though in 2012 he has been identified as Cefalu's new underboss.

Consigliere Joseph "Jo Jo" Corozzo – a former capo, Joseph and his brother Nicholas "Little Nick" Corozzo control the Queens-based "Corozzo faction". In 1992, Joseph became consigliere after Gotti's imprisonment. On February 8, 2008, Joseph and Nicholas were indicted during Operation Old Bridge. In June 2008, Joseph pleaded guilty to a racketeering conspiracy charge concerning the extortion of a Staten Island concrete firm and was sentenced to 46 months in prison. In 2011, Corozzo was indicted on new federal racketeering charges. He currently has no release date.

Current family capos

During the 1980s and 90s, the Gambino crime family under boss John Gotti, Sr. had 24 active crews operating in New York City, New Jersey, South Florida, and Connecticut. After 2000, the Gambino family had approximately 20 crews. However, according to a 2004 New Jersey Organized Crime Report, the Gambino family had only ten active crews.

New York

Brooklyn/Staten Island faction

Anthony "Sonny" Ciccone – Capo of the Gambino crew on the Brooklyn waterfront. Currently imprisoned on several extortion charges. Was released from prison on April 24, 2013.

George "Butters" DeCicco – Capo of a Staten Island and Brooklyn crew since the 1980s. The brother of former underboss Frank DeCicco, George is heavily involved in loansharking.

Joseph "Sonny" Juliano – Capo of a Brooklyn crew that operates illegal gambling, loansharking, fraud and wire fraud activities. Juliano previously managed a multimillion dollar illegal gambling ring in 30 New York City locations.

Francesco "Frank" Cali – Capo who operates in Manhattan, Brooklyn and New Jersey. According to the FBI, Cali is the official Gambino "ambassador to the Sicilian Mafia" and a rising star in the crime family. Cali and Leonard DiMaria extorted money from businessman Joseph Vollaro's trucking company on Staten Island. A major suspect in the drug trafficking between the Sicilian Mafia and the Gambinos, Cali pleaded guilty to racketeering charges and was sent to prison. He was released on May 30, 2009.

Pasquale Conte – Capo in the Sicilian faction which operates in Brooklyn and Staten Island.

Carmine Sciandra – Capo of a crew in Staten Island who also co-owns three "Top Tomato" vegetable and fruit markets. In December 2005, Sciandra was shot and wounded by a retired policeman while working at his Staten Island market. On March 25, 2010, Sciandra plead guilty to state charges of enterprise corruption and grand larceny for running a massive sports betting and loan shark operation and was sentenced to serve between 1½ to 4½ years in prison. He was released on January 5, 2012.

Louis "Big Lou" Vallario – Capo of a crew in Bensonhurst, Brooklyn since the 1980s. From 1996 to 2002, Vallario served as acting boss in the family's 'Ruling Committee/Panel. One of the last aides to John Gotti. He was released on October 15, 2013.

Queens faction

Thomas "Tommy Sneakers" Cacciopoli – Capo of a crew in Queens, New Jersey, and Westchester. Released from prison on April 4, 2011.

Manhattan faction

Salvatore "Mr. Sal" Franco- Capo of a Manhattan crew.

Joseph "Joe the Blond" Giordano – Capo of a Manhattan and Long Island crew.

Joseph "Joe" Lombardi – Capo of a Manhattan and Staten Island crew.

Vincent "Vinny Butch" Corrao – Capo of a Little Italy, Manhattan crew. Vincent's grandfather, "Vinny the Shrimp", operated the same crew and passed it to his son Joseph Corrao. Joseph later passed the crew to his son Vincent.

Bronx faction

Salvatore "Tore" LoCascio – Capo of a Bronx crew and son of Frank "Frankie Loc" LoCascio. Along with Richard Martino, Salvatore introduced the Gambinos to online pornography operations that earned the family up to $350 million per year. In 2003, Salvatore was convicted and sent to prison. On August 1, 2008, Salvatore was released from prison.

Louis "Louie Bracciole" Ricco – Capo of a crew in the Bronx, Brooklyn, and New Jersey. The crew controls half of the illegal gambling, loansharking and racketeering activities in the Bronx.

Sicilian faction

The Sicilian faction of the Gambino crime family is known as the *Cherry Hill Gambinos*. Gambino Boss Carlo Gambino created an alliance between the Gambino family and three Sicilian clans: the *Inzerillo's*, the *Spatola's* and the *Di Maggio's*. Carlo Gambino's relatives controlled the *Inzerillo clan* under Salvatore Inzerillo in Passo di Ragano, a neighborhood in Palermo, Sicily. Salvatore Inzerillo coordinated the major heroin trafficking from Sicily to the US, bringing his cousins John, Giuseppe and Rosario Gambino to the US to supervise the operation. The

Gambino brothers ran a Cafe on 18th Avenue in Bensonhurst and took their name *"Cherry Hill Gambinos"* from Cherry Hill, New Jersey. The Gambino family in America began increasing in size with more Sicilian members.

Giovanni "John" Gambino – Capo in the Gambino Sicilian or *Zip* faction. Gambino is an Italian national who belongs to the Inzerillo-Gambino-DiMaggio-Spatola clan of Sicily as well as the Gambino family. Reputedly a prominent drug trafficker, Gambino allegedly participates in the three-man ruling panel/committee that runs the crime family.

New Jersey

In Northern New Jersey, the Gambino family operates crews in Bergen, Passaic, and Essex Counties. In Southern New Jersey, the family operates crews in South Trenton, and Atlantic City. The two Gambino crews operating in New Jersey are the *Mitarotonda crew* and the *Sisca crew*. Other capos operating in New Jersey include John D'Amico, Louis Ricco, Francesco Cali, and Thomas Cacciopoli.

Alphonse "Funzi" Sisca – Capo of a crew in New Jersey. He was a John Gotti ally and a former drug dealing partner of Angelo Ruggiero and Arnold Squitieri. Prior to being convicted in 2006, Sisca had spent 20 of the past 30 years in prison. He was released from prison on September 27, 2010.

Nicholas Mitarotonda – capo of a crew in Elizabeth, New Jersey. Mitarotonda was released from federal prison on March 1, 2011.

Florida

The Gambino family's Florida faction operates in Tampa and the South Florida counties of Broward, Palm Beach and Dade.

Freddy Massaro – Capo of a South Florida crew. Massaro also owns Beachside Mario's, a restaurant in Sunny Isles Beach.

Leonard "Lenny" DiMaria — Capo of a South Florida crew.

Atlanta, Georgia

Steven Kaplan, a family associate was the manager of the Gold Club a strip club in Atlanta, he employed women to provide sexual services in his club.

Soldiers

Blaise Corozzo – Soldier and another of the Corozzo brothers. He is serving a one- to three-year sentence in state prison for a 2008 illegal gambling operation. His son Nicholas Corozzo, also involved with the Gambino family, was arrested in 2004. In 2009, Blaise Corozzo was released from prison.

Andrew "Andy Campo" Campos – soldier and former acting capo of the Bronx-based LoCascio crew. Campos supervised Tore LoCascio's crew while he was in prison.

Michael Murdocco – Soldier in Carmine Sciandra's crew. Murdocco and his son-in-law Sanitation Deputy Chief Frederick Grimaldi, rigged bids to help a New Jersey firm win a sanitation contract. In exchange for kickbacks, Grimaldi allegedly leaked bid information to Murdocco in May 2009. Currently serving two to six years in state prison after pleading guilty in March 2010 to enterprise corruption, grand larceny and receiving bribes. Murdocco was paroled on July 7, 2012.

Rosario Spatola – member of the *Cherry Hill Gambinos*. His cousin is Giovanni "John" Gambino and his brother-in-law was Salvatore Inzerillo.

Imprisoned members

Andrew Merola – former acting capo of the Mitarotonda crew. Merola is connected to Lucchese crime family Jersey faction leader Martin Taccetta. Merola's crew operates illegal gambling, loansharking, extortion and labor racketeering. Pleaded guilty to racketeering conspiracy and was sentenced to 11 years in prison. His projected release date is June 5, 2020.

Daniel "Danny" Marino – Capo of a Queens crew involved in labor and construction racketeering. A rival of John Gotti, Marino was involved in the 1986 murder conspiracy that accidentally killed Frank DeCicco instead of Gotti.

Bartolomeo "Bobby" Vernace – Capo of a Queens crew. Vernace allegedly operates out of his Vita Cafe in Flushing, Queens, running illegal gambling activities. Vernace is currently being held at the Metropolitan Detention Center in Brooklyn while awaiting trial.

Vincent "Little Vinny" Artuso – capo of a crew in Broward County, Fort Lauderdale, Palm Beach County, Boca Raton and Palm Beach Island. Artuso lives in South Palm Beach, Florida. On January 22, 2008 in Fort Lauderdale, Artuso was charged with racketeering. In September 2008, Artuso was charged with racketeering, mail and wire fraud, and money laundering. Artuso is currently imprisoned at the Coleman Federal Correctional Complex in Florida; his projected release date is August 28, 2016. His son, John Vincent Artuso, is also imprisoned at Coleman; his release date is July 29, 2016.

Anthony "Tony Genius" Megale – Capo of the Connecticut faction and co-leader with Domenico Cefalu of the Sicilian faction. In 2002, Megale was named acting underboss after Peter Gotti went to prison. His projected release date is July 18, 2014.

Augustus Sclafani – former acting capo of the Corrao crew. Sclafani was the overseer of the crew while Corrao was imprisoned, but Sclafani came under indictment in 2008 Operation Old Bridge and is currently in prison.

Nicholas "Little Nick" Corozzo – Capo. Brother of Consigliere Joseph Corozzo, uncle of Joseph, Jr. and currently the most influential Caporegime in the crime family. Became a fugitive for almost four months, currently incarcerated on a 13 year sentence. His projected release date is March 2, 2020.

Dominick "Skinny Dom" Pizzonia – Capo of a crew in Queens. An enforcer and hitman with John Gotti, Pizzonia is currently serving a 15-year-sentence for gambling and loansharking conspiracy. His projected release date is on February 28, 2020.

Crews

Ciccone Crew

Waterfront Crew

Franco Crew

Sisca Crew

The Ozone Park Boys

Cherry Hill Gambinos (headed by John Gambino)

Howard Beach Crew

Defunct

Baltimore Crew

Alliances with other criminal groups

The Gambino-Lucchese-Genovese alliance (1953–1985) between Carlo Gambino, Tommy Lucchese, and Vito Genovese began with a plot to take over the Mafia Commission by murdering family bosses Frank Costello and Albert Anastasia. At that time, Gambino was Anastasia's new underboss and Vito Genovese was the underboss for Costello. Their first target was Costello on May 2, 1957. Costello survived the assassination attempt, but immediately decided to retire as boss in favor of Genovese. Their second target was Anastasia on October 25, 1957. The Gallo brothers (from the Colombo family) murdered Anastasia in a Manhattan barber shop, opening the war for Gambino to become the new boss of the now-Gambino crime family. After assuming power, Gambino started conspiring with Lucchese to remove their former ally Genovese. In 1959, with the assistance of Luciano, Costello, and Meyer Lansky, Genovese was arrested and Gambino assumed full control with Lucchese of the Mafia Commission. Under Gambino and Lucchese, the Commission pushed Bonanno boss Joseph Bonanno out of power, triggering an internal war in that family. In the 1960s, the Commission backed the Gallo brothers in their rebellion against Profaci family boss Joe Profaci. In 1962, Gambino's oldest son Thomas married Lucchese's daughter, strengthening the Gambino and Lucchese family alliance. Lucchese gave Gambino access into the New York airports rackets he controlled, and Gambino allowed Lucchese into some of their rackets. After Lucchese death in July 1967, Gambino used his power over the Commission to appoint Carmine Tramunti as the new Lucchese family leader. Gambino later continued the alliance with Tramunti's successor, Anthony Corallo. After Gambino's death, new Gambino boss Paul Castellano continued the Lucchese alliance. In 1985, the original Gambino-Lucchese alliance dissolved when John Gotti ordered Castellano's assassination and took power in the Gambino family without Commission approval.

The Gambino-Lucchese alliance (1999–present) was initiated by acting Lucchese boss Steven Crea in 1999. The two families extorted the construction industry and made millions of dollars in bid-rigging. In early 2002, Lucchese Capo John Capra worked with Gambino acting Boss Arnold Squitieri, acting underboss Anthony Megale, and Bronx-based acting Capo Gregory DePalma. The group was involved in illegal gambling and extortion activities in Westchester County, New York. The members were arrested in 2005 leaving to reveal that Gambino acting Capo DePalma had allowed an FBI agent Joaquin Garcia (known as Jack Falcone) work undercover with his crew since 2002. In late 2008, Gambino family acting Capo Andrew Merola teamed with Lucchese Jersey faction acting Boss Martin Taccetta in an illegal gambling ring, shaking down unions, and extorting car dealerships. Merola was indicted in 2008 and Taccetta was returned to prison in 2009.

The Gambino-Genovese alliance (1962–1972) was between Carlo Gambino and Genovese family acting boss/front boss Tomas Eboli. The alliance was short-lived because Eboli was unable or unwilling to repay Gambino money from a bad narcotics deal. The alliance ended when Gambino ordered Eboli's murder on July 16, 1972.

The Gambino-Bonanno alliance (1991–2004) started with John Gotti and new Bonanno boss Joseph Massino. As a member of the Mafia Commission, Gotti helped Massino regain the Bonanno commission seat that was lost in the early 1970s. The Gambino family influenced the Bonanno family to give up narcotics trafficking and return to more traditional Cosa Nostra crimes (loan sharking, gambling, stock fraud, etc.) By the late 1990s, the Bonannos had become almost as strong as the Gambinos.

The Gambino-Westies alliance (1970s-present) This alliance resulted from an ongoing war between the Genovese family and the Westies, an Irish-American street gang in the Hell's Kitchen section of Manhattan. Genovese front boss Anthony "Fat Tony" Salerno wanted to seize control of lucrative construction rackets at the new Jacob Javits Convention Center from the Westies. When the Westies balked, Salerno ordered the murder of the top gang leaders. Eventually, the Genovese family invited the Gambinos to broker a peace agreement with the Westside Gang. As part of this agreement, the Westies formed an alliance with Gambino capo Roy DeMeo.

Government informants
And witnesses

Salvatore "Sammy the Bull" Gravano, Underboss

Michael "Mikey Scars" DiLeonardo, Caporegime

Dominic "Fat Dom" Borghese, Soldier

Frank "Frankie Fap" Fappiano, Soldier

Willie Boy Johnson, Associate

Dominick "Big Dom" LoFaro, Associate

Frank "Red" Scollo, Gambino-associated union official

Andrew DiDonato Associate

Robert Mormando, Soldier

Lewis Kasman, associate, and self-described "adopted son" of John Gotti who first became an informant in 1996 Was dropped from testifying against John Gotti, Jr. for unreliability, but nevertheless received only probation for his offenses at sentencing.

Gambino family mobsters

Anthony "Tough Tony" Anastasio (Major racketeer in New York)

Carmine Agnello

Bartholomew "Bobby" Boriello

Louis Capone (Worked under Albert Anastasia in the Murder Inc. organisation)

Roy DeMeo (Ran the DeMeo crew)

William "Billy Batts" Devino

Carmine "Charley Wagons" Fatico

Carmine "Doctor" Lombardozzi

Ralph "Ralphie Bones" Mosca

Frank Piccolo

Angelo "Quack Quack" Ruggiero

Anthony Scotto

Trials involving Gambino family

Mafia Commission Trial

Pizza Connection Trial

In popular culture

Witness to the Mob – A made-for-television movie about the life of Gambino underboss turned FBI informant Sammy Gravano.

In the 2001 TV movie, *Boss of Bosses*, actor Chazz Palminteri portrays Gambino boss Paul Castellano.

In the 1996 TV movie *Gotti*, actor Armand Assante portrays Gambino boss John Gotti .

In the movie *Goodfellas*, Gambino family made member William "Billy Batts" DeVino (played by Frank Vincent) is killed in a fight with Thomas DeSimone (portrayed as "Tommy DeVito" by Joe Pesci) a Lucchese crime family associate.

In the video game GTA IV, in which the setting is based on New York and New Jersey, the Gambetti family is a reference to the Gambinos. Also during the mission "Waste Not Want Knots" en route to a Mafia controlled waste management plant Michael Keane (a character) mentions the Gambinos while reciting numerous fictional and real Mafia families.

Law & Order commonly references the Gambinos as a literary flourish but does not involve actual persons except to allude to them by the court cases that were inspired by actual events, commonly 'Ripped from the headlines'. The character of Frank Masucci and the Masucci crime family were based on John Gotti and the Gambino crime family.

In *Frasier* season 4 episode 23, Frasier tells Daphne and Martin "It's like Christmas morning in the Gambino's household", at the end of their argument regarding their exchange of gifts.

Genovese crime family

The **Genovese crime family** is one of the "Five Families" that dominate organized crime activities in New York City as part of the Mafia (or *Cosa Nostra*). The Genovese crime family has been nicknamed the "Ivy League" and "Rolls Royce" of organized crime. They are rivaled in size only by the Gambino crime family and are unmatched in terms of power. They have generally maintained a varying degree of influence over many of the smaller mob families outside of New York, including ties with the Patriarca, Buffalo and Philadelphia crime families.

Finding new ways to make money in the 21st century, the Genovese family took advantage of lax due diligence by banks during the housing spike with a wave of mortgage frauds. Prosecutors say loan shark victims obtained home equity loans to pay off debts to their mob bankers. The family found ways to use new technology to improve on illegal gambling, with customers placing bets through offshore sites via the Internet.

Lucky Luciano

The current "family" was founded by Lucky Luciano, but in 1957 it was renamed after boss Vito Genovese. Originally in control of the waterfront on the West Side of Manhattan (including the Fulton Fish Market), the family was run for years by "the Oddfather", Vincent "the Chin" Gigante, who feigned insanity by shuffling unshaven through New York's Greenwich Village wearing a tattered bath robe and muttering to himself incoherently.

Although the leadership of the Genovese family seemed to have been in limbo after the death of Gigante in 2005, they appear to be the most organized family and remain powerful. Unique in today's Mafia, the family has benefited greatly from members following the code of Omertà. While many mobsters from across the country have testified against their crime families since the 1980s, the Genovese family has only had six members turn state's evidence in its history.

Origins

Giuseppe Morello

The Genovese crime family originated from the Morello crime family of East Harlem, the first Mafia family in New York City. In 1892, Giuseppe Morello arrived in New York from the village of Corleone, Sicily, when only a few thousand Italians lived in New York. Morello's half-brothers Nicholas, Vincenzo, Ciro and the rest of his family joined him in New York the following year. The Morello brothers formed the 107th Street Mob and began dominating the Italian neighborhood of East Harlem, parts of Manhattan, and the Bronx.

One of Giuseppe Morello's strongest allies was Ignazio "the Wolf" Lupo, a mobster who controlled Little Italy, Manhattan. In 1903, Lupo married Morello's half-sister, uniting both organizations. The Morello-Lupo alliance continued to prosper in 1903, when the group began a major counterfeiting ring with powerful Sicilian Mafioso *Don* Vito Cascio Ferro, printing $5 bills in Sicily and smuggling them into the United States. New York City Police detective Joseph Petrosino began investigating the Morello family's counterfeiting operation, the barrel murders and the black hand extortion letters. On November 15, 1909 Giuseppe Morello, Ignazio Lupo and others were arrested on counterfeiting charges. In February 1910, Morello and Lupo were sentenced to 30 years in prison.

As the Morello family increased in power and influence, bloody territorial conflicts arose with other Italian criminal gangs in New York. The Morellos had an alliance with Giosue Gallucci, a prominent East Harlem businessman and Camorrista with local political connections. On May 17, 1915 Gallucci was murdered in a power struggle between the Morello's and the Neapolitan Camorra organization, which consisted of two Brooklyn gangs run by Pellegrino Morano and Alessandro Vollero. The fight over Gallucci's rackets became known as the Mafia-

Camorra War. After months of fighting, Camorra boss Morano offered a truce to end the fighting. A meeting was arranged at a Navy Street cafe owned by Alessandro Vollero. On September 7, 1916 upon arriving, Nicholas "Nick" Morello and his bodyguard Charles Ubriaco were ambushed by five members of the Brooklyn Camorra group and killed In 1917, Morano was charged with Morello's murder after Camorrista Ralph Daniello implicated him in the murder. By 1918, law enforcement had sent many Camorra gang members to prison, decimating the Camorra in New York and ending the war. Many of the remaining Brooklyn Camorra gang members joined the Morello family.

The Morellos now faced stronger rivals than the Camorra. With the passage of Prohibition in 1919 and the outlawing of alcohol sales, the Morello family regrouped and built a lucrative bootlegging operation in Manhattan. In 1920, both Giuseppe Morello and Ignazio Lupo were released from prison and Brooklyn Mafia Boss Salvatore D'Aquila ordered their murders. This is when Joseph Masseria and Rocco Valenti, a former Brooklyn Camorra began to fight for control of the Morello family. On December 29, 1920 Masseria's men murdered Valenti's ally, Salvatore Mauro. Then on May 8, 1922, the Valenti gang murdered Vincenzo Terranova. Masseria's gang retaliated killing Silva Tagliagamba. On August 11, 1922, Masseria's men murdered Valenti ending the conflict. Masseria won and essentially took over the Morello family.

The Castellammarese era

Joe Masseria

During the mid-1920s, Massaria continued to expand his bootlegging, extortion, loansharking, and illegal gambling rackets throughout New York. To operate and protect these rackets, Massaria recruited many ambitious young mobsters. These mobsters included future Cosa Nostra powers Charlie "Lucky" Luciano, Frank Costello, Joseph "Joey A" Adonis, Vito Genovese, and Albert Anastasia. Masseria was willing to take all Italian-American recruits, no matter where they had originated in Sicily or Italy.

Masseria's strongest rival in New York was Salvatore Maranzano, leader of the Castellammare del Golfo Sicilian organization in Brooklyn. A recent arrival from Sicily, Maranzano had strong support from elements of the Sicilian Mafia and was a traditionalist mafiosi. He recruited Sicilian mobsters only, preferably from the Castellammarese clan. Maranzano's top lieutenants included future family bosses Joseph "Joe Bananas" Bonanno, Joseph Profaci, and Stefano Magaddino. By 1928, the Castellammarese War between Masseria and Maranzano had begun. By the late 1920s, more than 60 mobsters on both sides had been murdered. On April 15, 1931, Masseria was murdered in a Coney Island, Brooklyn, restaurant, reportedly by members of Luciano's crew. Angry over broken promises from Masseria, Luciano had secretly conspired with Maranzano to plot Masseria's assassination. On the day of the murder, Luciano was allegedly eating dinner with Masseria at a restaurant. After Luciano went to the restroom, his hitmen arrived and murdered Masseria. With Masseria's death, the Castellamarese War had ended.

Now in control of New York, Maranzano took several important steps to solidify his victory. He reorganized the Italian-American gangs of New York into five new families, structured after the hierarchical and highly disciplined Mafia families of Sicily. Maranzano's second big change was to appoint himself as the boss of all the families. As part of this reorganization, Maranzano designated Luciano as boss of the old Morello/Masseria family. However, Luciano and other mob leaders privately objected to Maranzano's dictatorial role. Maranzano soon found out about Luciano's discontent and ordered his assassination. Discovering that he was in danger, Luciano plotted Maranzano's assassination with Maranzano trustee Gaetano "Tommy" Lucchese. On September 10, 1931, Jewish gangsters provided by Luciano ally Meyer Lansky shot and stabbed Maranzano to death in his Manhattan office. Luciano was now the most powerful mobster in the United States.

Lucky

New York's Genovese crime family, the largest and most influential crime family in the United States, may have been born with the swipe of a knife over a clean-shaven cheek that left a lasting scar and an incentive for the man who received it, Charles, Lucky Luciano.

Charles "Lucky" Luciano

Over the years Luciano told several stories about how he got his nickname and the cut on his right cheek that caused his eye to droop. According to one such tale, kidnappers had tied him up and held him hostage, demanding inside information about a large drug shipment that was coming into New York City. In another version the scar was a present from a policeman who believed Lucky had acted inappropriately with one of his daughters. Either of these might be true, but the story that makes the most sense given Luciano's career in crime claims that in 1929 a gang of thugs sent by Mafia boss Salvatore Maranzano captured Luciano, tied him up, hung him by his arms from the rafters, and tortured him. Maranzano certainly had motive.

From Maranzano's point of view, Luciano didn't know his place. He was smart and ambitious, and unlike the small-minded Moustache Petes who ran the Mafia in America in the early part of the 20th century, Luciano had vision. Maranzano felt threatened.

Salvatore Maranzano

Petty rackets were for suckers, Luciano believed, and the Sicilian immigrant's suspicion and distrust of all non-Sicilians was counterproductive to the real goal of organized crime: making money. Maranzano and his chief moustache Pete rival, Giuseppe Joe the Boss Masseria wanted to keep their organizations exclusively for Sicilians. Luciano by contrast saw a role for all the ethnic crime groups in America, particularly the Jewish gangs. Why have dozens of squabbling local gangs when a nationwide syndicate with central authority could pool resources and turn criminal enterprise into big business? Putting together a national syndicate was Luciano's dream.

Luciano's positive feelings about the worth of non-Sicilians stemmed from his childhood. Born Salvatore Lucania outside of Palermo, Sicily, Luciano came to New York City as a boy. He started his first racket when he was still in elementary school. For a penny or two a day, Carl Sifakis writes in *The Mafia Encyclopedia,* Luciano offered younger and smaller Jewish kids his personal protection against beatings on the way to school; if they didn't pay, he beat them up. But one scrawny, little Jewish boy from Poland defied him, and when Luciano tried to carry out his threat of violence, the kid put up a fight and showed that he was a lot tougher than he looked. Luciano was impressed. He asked the boy what his name was. Maier Suchowljansky, the boy said. Years later he would shorten his name to Meyer Lansky, and he and Luciano would form a partnership that would revolutionize crime in America.

Luciano and

The Commission

"Lucky" Luciano's mugshot.

After Maranzano's murder, Luciano created a new governing body for the Cosa Nostra families, the Commission. The Commission consisted of representatives from each of the Five Families, the Chicago Outfit and the Magaddino crime family of Buffalo, New York. Luciano wanted the Commission to mediate disputes between the families and prevent future gang wars. Although nominally a democratic body, Luciano and his allies actually controlled the Commission throughout the 1930s. As head of the new Luciano family, Luciano appointed Vito Genovese as his underboss, or second in command, and Frank Costello as his Consigliere, or advisor. With the new structure in place, the five New York families would enjoy several decades of peace and growth.

Giuseppe Masseria

Masseria's passing gave rival boss Salvatore Maranzano
unchallenged authority over the New York rackets. Luciano
made peace with Maranzano and was made his second-in-
command, put in charge of Masseria's men. Maranzano
was a bit more forward-thinking than Joe the Boss in that
he sought to organize the Sicilian gangsters in America into
five *borghati* or family villages. This was a step in the
direction Luciano favored, but it wasn't enough to satisfy
the ambitious young gangster. Sensing that Luciano would
be trouble, Maranzano paid the notorious Irish hitman
Vince Mad Dog Coll a down payment of $25,000 with a
promise of $25,000 more for the rubout of Luciano and his
top associate Vito Genovese. But Luciano had a spy within
Maranzano's organization, Tommy Lucchese, and when
Luciano learned of the contract on his life, he decided to
strike first.

Vince "Mad Dog" Coll

On September 10, 1931, Maranzano ordered Luciano and Genovese to come to his office. Fearing that they were being set up for the kill, Luciano dispatched his own team of hand-picked killers: four Jewish gangsters whose faces were unknown to Maranzano's people. The hit team went to Maranzano's office before Luciano's scheduled arrival and told the secretary that they were government agents sent to do a spot-check of the books. Tommy Lucchese made sure he was there to point out Maranzano to the hit men. After disarming Maranzano's bodyguards, two of the hitmen held the guards at bay in the outer office while the other two went into Maranzano's inner office where they shot and stabbed him. Their mission accomplished, the four assassins and Lucchese fled down the staircase. On their way down, they ran into Mad Dog Coll who was just arriving to get set up for the murders of Luciano and Genovese. Informed of Maranzano's bloody demise, Coll turned around and left a happy man, $25,000 richer with no work to be performed.

(For decades, journalists and mob scholars have cited September 10, 1931, as The Night of the Sicilian Vespers when scores of mobsters as many as 90 by some accounts were assassinated allegedly on orders from Luciano and Meyer Lansky in a mass purge to clear the decks for their takeover. Jerry Capeci in *The Complete Idiots Guide to the Mafia* credibly debunks this myth, proving that at most five gangsters tied to Maranzano died that day.)

Thomas E. Dewey

With Maranzano out of the way, Luciano was now free to put together the crime syndicate of his dreams with tentacles that reached across the country and covered lucrative rackets in labor manipulation, loan-sharking, gambling, drugs, prostitution, and boot-legging. The new syndicate's board of directors included such nefarious non-Sicilians as Frank Costello, Dutch Shultz, Joe Adonis, Louis Lepke, and Meyer Lansky. Luciano even toyed with the idea of dropping the syndicates Mafia affiliation but was dissuaded by Lansky who felt that the specter of the Mafia would help them keep people in line even though at one point the Jewish members outnumbered the Sicilians.

In 1935, Luciano was indicted on pandering charges by New York district attorney Thomas Dewey. Many observers believed that Luciano would never have directly involved himself with prostitutes, and that the case was fraudulent. During the trial, Luciano made a tactical mistake in taking the witness stand, where the prosecutor interrogated him for five hours about how he made his living. In 1936, Luciano was convicted and sentenced to 30 to 50 years in prison. Luciano supporters cried foul, claiming that the case was a frame based on the testimony of lying pimps and whores who were plea-bargaining themselves out of prison time. Ironically, Luciano personally found prostitution an odious pursuit, though he didn't seem to have any trouble sharing in its profits.

Although in prison, Luciano continued to run his crime family. His underboss Genovese now supervised the day-to-day family activities. In 1937, Genovese was indicted on murder charges and fled the country to Italy. After Genovese's departure, Costello became the new acting boss of the Luciano family.

The special prosecutor leading the charge against Luciano was Thomas E. Dewey who at the time didn't realize that Luciano had saved his life earlier that year when Dutch Schultz vowed to assassinate the pesky prosecutor. Luciano knew that this would be bad for business, bringing down the wrath of the government, but Schultz was unwilling to listen to reason from fellow syndicate members. To stop the Dutchman from carrying out the hit, Luciano had Schultz killed. He was gunned down as he stood at a urinal in the Palace Chop House and Tavern in Newark, N.J.

During World War II, federal agents asked Luciano for help in preventing enemy sabotage on the New York waterfront and other activities. Luciano agreed to help, but in reality provided insignificant assistance to the allied cause. After the end of the war, the arrangement with Luciano became public knowledge. To prevent further embarrassment, the government agreed to deport Luciano on condition that he never return to the United States. In 1946, Luciano was taken from prison and deported to Italy, never to return to the United States. Costello became the effective boss of the Luciano family.

Luciano, who had been running the syndicate from prison, knew that he would have a hard time maintaining control over his rackets from Italy, so he clandestinely moved his base of operations to Cuba. Eventually the U.S. government learned of his presence there and forced him to return to Italy. The man he left in charge of what would later become known as the Genovese family was part of the new breed of gangster, an Italian, but not a Sicilian, who preferred negotiation over conflict and for that reason became known as the Prime Minister of the mob.

Luciano later died on January 26, 1962 (aged 64) in Naples Italy.

J. Edgar Hoover

Even the nation's top crime fighter, J. Edgar Hoover, the first and longest-sitting director of the Federal Bureau of Investigation, was not immune to Costello's temptations. Hoover loved the racetrack. Though he swore that he never bet more than two dollars on a single horse, he was rumored to send agents to place larger bets for him. Whenever Costello knew that Hoover would be at the track, the Prime Minister would fix races and, using celebrity columnist Walter Winchell as go-between, make sure that the director knew what the sure bets were so that he could place his wagers accordingly. Perhaps this is why Hoover for many years maintained that the Mafia did not exist in America and the FBI had better things to do than chase down what he thought of as mere gamblers. Without serious scrutiny from the federal government, the syndicate flourished.

Tony Accardo

By the early 1940s, Costello had his hand in many enterprises. He went into partnership with Meyer Lansky to form jukebox and cigarette machine companies. He put together a coalition of gangsters to open a string of gambling parlors in Florida. He and Chicago syndicate underboss Tony Accardo started a bookmaking operation in Miami that raked in $10 million a year in profits. He and Bugsy Siegel explored illegal opportunities on the West Coast. Realizing Lucky Luciano's dream, Costello's reach stretched from sea to shining sea.

Known for his expensive suits and impeccable grooming (he would typically go to the barber shop at the Waldorf Astoria Hotel every morning for a trim), Costello was a man about town in New York City. He lived in a swank apartment building on Central Park West and kept an ex-showgirl mistress across the park on Fifth Avenue. He was so trendy he even saw a psychiatrist, Dr. Richard H. Hoffman, long before television character Tony Soprano skulked off to see his shrink. Costello had been seeing Dr. Hoffman for two years before the newspapers got wind of it. The psychiatrist told reporters that he had advised his patient to associate with a better class of people. Costello abruptly terminated his therapy, countering that it was he who had introduced Hoffman to a better class of people.

Frank Sinatra with mob leaders

In December 1946, Costello attended a mob convention in Havana, Cuba, called by Lucky Luciano, who had set up shop on the island just months after his deportation to Italy. Attendees included Vito Genovese, Joe Bonanno, Tommy Lucchese, Willie Moretti, Tampa boss Santo Trafficante, New Orleans boss Carlos Marcello, Tony Accardo and the three Fischetti brothers (Al Capone's cousins) from Chicago as well as Jewish gangsters Meyer Lansky, Moe Dalitz, Longy Zwillman, and Doc Stacher. Singer Frank Sinatra had been invited to perform at the Hotel Nacional where the gangsters were meeting, giving them all a pretense for being there. They'd all come, they said, to see Frank. At the conference, Luciano, backed up by Costello and Lansky, put forth a motion to ban narcotics trafficking from the syndicates portfolio. Luciano hoped that by getting the syndicate out of the drug trade, he would stand a better chance of convincing American officials to reverse his deportation order. But the bosses from around the country wouldn't agree to it. Drug dealing was just too lucrative to abandon, and one of its most vociferous proponents was Luciano's close associate, Vito Genovese.

At the Havana Conference Genovese revealed his ambitions to take over the syndicate. He lobbied to get Luciano to retire, asking Lucky in private if it might be time to step down while at the same time polling the other conference attendees to see if he could get them to vote Luciano out. Genovese also proposed that Albert Anastasia, the Lord High Executioner, be eliminated because he had become too kill crazy. Anastasia had been dropping hints that he was going to put a contract out on Bureau of Narcotics Director Harry Anslinger. Luciano called off the hit on Anslinger and managed to block Genovese's move to kill Anastasia, knowing that he would need the Lord High Executioners muscle if Genovese ever decided to go to war for supremacy of the New York rackets. The syndicate summit ended, and the mobsters, including Frank Costello, returned home with American officials none the wiser.

The Prime Minister

Frank Costello at the Kefauver hearings

During the reign of Frank Costello, the Luciano family controlled much of the bookmaking, loansharking, illegal gambling and labor racketeering activities in New York City. Costello wanted to increase the family involvement in lucrative financial schemes; he was less interested in low grossing criminal activities that relied on brutality and intimidation. Costello believed in diplomacy and discipline, and in diversifying family interests. Nicknamed "The Prime Minister of the Underworld", Costello controlled much of the New York waterfront and had tremendous political connections. It was said that no state judge could be appointed in any case without Costello's consent. During the 1940s, Costello allowed Luciano associates Meyer Lansky and Benjamin "Bugsy" Siegel to expand the family business in Southern California and build the first modern casino resort in Las Vegas. When Siegel failed to open the resort on time, his mob investors allegedly sanctioned his murder.

While serving as boss of the Luciano family in the 1950s, Costello suffered from depression and panic attacks. During this period Costello sought help from a psychiatrist, who advised him to distance himself from old associates such as Genovese and spend more time with politicians. In the early 1950s, U.S. Senator Estes Kefauver of Tennessee began investigating organized crime in New York in the Kefauver hearings. The Committee summoned numerous mobsters to testify, but they refused to answer questions at the hearings. The mobsters uniformly cited the Fifth Amendment of the U.S. Constitution, a legal protection against self-incrimination. However, when Costello was summoned, he agreed to answer questions at the hearings and not take the Fifth Amendment. As part of the agreement to testify, the Special Committee and the U.S. television networks agreed not to broadcast Costello's face. During the questioning, Costello nervously refused to answer certain questions and skirted around others. When the Committee asked Costello, "What have you done for your country Mr. Costello?" he famously replied, "Paid my tax!". The TV cameras, unable to show Costello's face, instead focused on his hands, which Costello wrung nervously while answering questions. Costello eventually walked out of the hearings.

In the end he was portrayed as a master manipulator who pulled the strings behind the scenes. His appearance before the committee exposed him for what he was and gradually weakened his effectiveness as a mob leader.

Abe Reles

Despite his reputation as an able negotiator, Frank Costello was not above using violence when he deemed it necessary, but when he did lash out, he did it his way. As Luciano's acting boss in New York, he sat on the syndicate commission that decided whether certain individuals should be executed. When Abe Kid Twist Reles, one of Murder Inc.'s top executioners, started cooperating with authorities, Costello is said to have found out through his police sources where Reles was being kept, the Half Moon Hotel in Coney Island. Despite a cadre of detectives guarding Reles, someone managed to get into his room and push him out a window to his death. The details of the murder remain a mystery, but all those involved at the time agree that it was Costello who pulled the strings to make it happen.

On May 2, 1957, a black Cadillac quietly pulled up to the curb outside Costello's Manhattan apartment building just as he was walking in. A 300-pound man emerged from the car, rushed into the lobby, and hid behind a pillar, a gun in his hand. This is for you, Frank, the fat man shouted.

Costello turned toward the voice just as the gun went off. The fat man ran back to the Cadillac, not realizing that the bullet had only grazed Costello's scalp above his ear. The wound was minor and Costello survived, but the incident convinced him that retirement might be in his best interests. The rotund shooter was alleged to be Vincent Chin Gigante who immediately went into hiding and lost a considerable amount of weight before turning himself in. Gigante stood trial for the shooting, but when the prosecutor asked Costello on the stand to identify the man who wounded him, the boss obeyed the rules of *omerta,* the Mafia vow of secrecy and claimed that he had never set eyes on Gigante. As a result, Gigante was acquitted on all charges.

Costello after assassination attempt

The mob commission allowed Costello to retire quietly and keep the income from his rackets. Waiting in the wings to take his place was Vito Genovese who had been angling for years to become boss of the organization Lucky Luciano had put together. Genovese, who demanded that his underlings refer to him as Don Vito, was as vicious as he was clever. His goal was to be anointed Boss of all Bosses.

On November 14, 1957, just 20 days after the attempt on Frank Costello's life, 58 mobsters from across the country assembled in the rural upstate New York town of Apalachin. Vito Genovese had pushed for the Apalachin Conference, as it later became known, and it's generally believed that this was where he planned to have himself crowned boss of all bosses.

At this time the syndicate still hadn't made up its mind about narcotics. On the one hand, mobsters saw almost limitless profit potential in dealing drugs, but many of the bosses also recognized the risks. Authorities could look the other way when it came to gambling or prostitution, but government officials at least the ones who hadn't already been corrupted by the mob were hell-bent on squashing illegal drug use in the United States. Lucky Luciano, among others, felt that the narcotics trade would result in prosecutions and convictions that no amount of bribery could prevent and eventually the syndicate's dominance over the underworld would erode.

Don Vito Genovese, however, could not resist the riches that drugs produced, and he, more than any other mob leader, wanted to expand the syndicate's involvement in narcotics. Luciano and Lansky felt that this would destroy all that they'd built, so together with Frank Costello, who was hungry for a taste of that cold delicacy called revenge, they plotted to bring down Genovese. They invited Carlo Gambino, who now headed the family formerly controlled by Albert Anastasia, into their conspiracy. Genovese mistakenly thought of Gambino as a solid ally because he had helped the foxy Gambino eliminate Anastasia.

The gangsters invited to the Apalachin Conference, most of them supporters of Genovese, gathered at a stone mansion owned by a local businessman named Joseph Barbara who had sent his wife out the day before to pick up enough steaks to feed a small army. Shiny luxury cars jammed the driveway and lined the road outside Barbara's 58-acre estate. Inside the house the mobsters were getting comfortable, settling in for their meeting.

Joseph Barbara estate

Suddenly, a cadre of New York State troopers raided the house. The mobsters fled in panic, some running across the fields that surrounded the house in their fancy suits and shiny wingtips, desperate to get to the woods where they hoped they could escape. Others, like Genovese, jumped into their cars and sped off only to be stopped by police road blocks. Dozens of ex-cons and known criminals were apprehended. Many accounts of the incident credit the diligent efforts of a perceptive state trooper named Edgar Croswell who had noticed suspicious cars coming in and out of the area, but it was more likely that the authorities were tipped off by individuals hired by Luciano, Costello, and Lansky, none of whom appeared at the conference. Luciano was forbidden from entering the country. Costello claimed that he was under constant police surveillance and couldn't slip away undetected. Lansky called in sick and stayed home in Florida. Vito Genovese and Carlo Gambino were among the mobsters arrested.

Meyer Lansky mugshot

Genovese had been dealt a blow, but he was by no means out of the picture, and now that his enemies had kicked the hornets' nest, they had to eliminate the problem before they got stung. Luciano, Lansky, and Costello knew that Genovese would be gunning for them, so they put together another plot, hoping to eliminate him before he eliminated them, and they used the bait that Genovese just couldn't resist. After setting up a lucrative drug deal that was just too good for Genovese to pass up, they paid a Puerto Rican drug dealer named Nelson Melon Cantellops $100,000 to turn states witness and testify against Genovese. Luciano, Costello, and Lansky fed Cantellops choice insider information to boost his credibility. The Melon told a grand jury in Manhattan that he had attended a meeting at which Genovese conspired to take over the entire drug trade in the Bronx. Prosecutors chose to ignore the fact that in all probability a small-fish drug pusher wouldn't have had access to a big-fish Mafia boss and that whatever testimony he gave would be hearsay at best, but they wanted Genovese so badly, they took the little fish's testimony as gospel truth and won a conviction against Genovese on April 17, 1959. Genovese was given a 15-year sentence.

Joseph Valachi testifies

The imprisoned Don Vito continued to rule the family, which now bore his name (thanks to the testimony of turncoat Joseph Valachi who publicly referred to it as such), using his brother Mike as his messenger. Vito Genovese died of a heart attack on February 14, 1969, at the federal prison medical center in Springfield, Mo.

The return of Genovese

Costello ruled for 20 peaceful years, but that quiet reign
ended when Genovese was extradited from Italy to New
York. During his absence, Costello demoted Genovese
from underboss to capo and Genovese determined to take
control of the family. Soon after his arrival in the United
States, Genovese was acquitted of the 1936 murder charge
that had driven him into exile. Free of legal entanglements,
Genovese started plotting against Costello with the
assistance of Mangano crime family underboss Carlo
Gambino. On May 2, 1957, Luciano family mobster
Vincent "Chin" Gigante shot Costello in the side of the
head on a public street; however, Costello survived the
attack. Months later, Mangano family boss Albert
Anastasia, a powerful ally of Costello, was murdered by
Gambino's gunmen. With Anastasia's death, Gambino
seized control of the Mangano family. Feeling afraid and
isolated after the shootings, Costello quietly retired and
surrendered control of the Luciano family to Genovese.

Vito Genovese's mugshot

Having taken control of what was now the Genovese crime family in 1957, Vito Genovese decided to organize a Cosa Nostra conference to legitimize his new position. Held on mobster Joseph Barbara's farm in Apalachin, New York, the Apalachin Meeting attracted over 100 Cosa Nostra mobsters from around the nation. However, local law enforcement discovered the meeting by chance and quickly surrounded the farm. As the meeting broke up, Genovese escaped capture by running through the woods. However, many other high-ranking mobsters were arrested. Cosa Nostra leaders were chagrined by the public exposure and bad publicity from the Apalachin meeting, and generally blamed Genovese for the fiasco. Wary of Genovese gaining more power in the Mafia Commission, Gambino used the abortive Apalachin Meeting as an excuse to move against his former ally. Gambino, former Genovese bosses Lucky Luciano and Frank Costello, and Lucchese crime family boss Tommy Lucchese allegedly lured Genovese into a drug distribution scheme that ultimately resulted in his conspiracy indictment and conviction. In 1959, Genovese was sentenced to 15 years in prison on narcotics charges. Genovese, who was the most powerful boss in New York, had been effectively eliminated as a rival by Gambino. Genovese would later die in prison.

The Valachi Hearings

The Genovese family was soon rocked by a second public embarrassment: the United States Senate McClellan Hearings. While incarcerated at a federal prison in Atlanta, Genovese soldier Joseph "Joe Cargo" Valachi believed he was being targeted for murder by the mob on the suspicion that he was an informer. On June 22, 1962, Valachi brutally murdered another inmate with a pipe. Valachi told investigators that he thought the victim was Joseph "Joe Beck" DiPalermo, a Lucchese soldier coming to kill him.

To avoid a capital murder trial, Valachi agreed to cooperate with federal prosecutors against the Genovese family. He thus became the first Cosa Nostra mobster to publicly affirm the organization's existence. With information from prosecutors, the low-level Valachi was able to testify in nationally-televised hearings about the Cosa Nostra's influence over legal enterprises in aid of racketeering and other criminal activities to make huge profit. Valachi also introduced the name "Cosa Nostra" as a household name. Although Valachi's testimony never led to any convictions, it helped law enforcement by identifying many members of the Genovese and other New York families.

Front bosses

And

The ruling panels

After Genovese was sent to prison in 1959, the family leadership secretly established a "Ruling Panel" to run the family in Genovese's absence. This first panel included acting boss Thomas "Tommy Ryan" Eboli, underboss Gerardo "Jerry" Catena, and Catena's protégé Philip "Benny Squint" Lombardo. After Genovese died in 1969, Lombardo was named his successor. However, the family appointed a series of "Front Bosses" to masquerade as the official family boss.

The aim of these deceptions was to protect Lombardo by confusing law enforcement about who was the true leader of the family. In the late 1960s, Gambino boss Carlo Gambino loaned $4 million to Eboli for a drug scheme in an attempt to gain control of the Genovese family. When Eboli failed to pay back his debt, Gambino, with Commission approval, murdered Eboli in 1972.

After Eboli's death, Genovese capo and Gambino ally Frank "Funzi" Tieri was appointed as the new front boss. In reality, the Genovese family created a new ruling panel to run the family. This second panel consisted of Catena, Michele "Big Mike" Miranda, and Lombardo. In 1981, Tieri became the first Cosa Nostra boss to be convicted under the new Racketeer Influenced and Corrupt Organizations Act (RICO). In 1982, Tieri died in prison. After Tieri went to prison in 1981, the Genovese family reshuffled its leadership. The capo of the Manhattan faction, Anthony Salerno ("Fat Tony"), became the new front boss. Lombardo, the defacto boss of the family, retired and Vincent "Chin" Gigante, the triggerman on the failed Costello hit, took actual control of the family. In 1985, Salerno was convicted in the Mafia Commission Trial and sentenced to 100 years in federal prison.

After the 1980 murder of Philadelphia crime family boss Angelo "Gentle Don" Bruno, Gigante and Lombardo began manipulating the rival factions in the war-torn Philadelphia family. Gigante and Lombardo finally gave their support to Philadelphia mobster Nicodemo "Little Nicky" Scarfo, who in return gave the Genovese mobsters permission to operate in Atlantic City in 1982.

The Oddfather

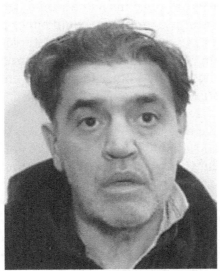

FBI mugshot of Vincent Gigante in his bathrobe

Gigante was even more concerned about keeping law enforcement at bay than Lombardo had been. His best-known tactic to confuse law enforcement was by pretending insanity. Gigante frequently walked down New York streets in a bathrobe, mumbling incoherently. Gigante succeeded in convincing court-appointed psychiatrists that his mental illness was worsening, and avoided several criminal prosecutions. The New York media soon nicknamed Gigante "The Oddfather". Gigante reportedly operated from the Triangle Social Club in Greenwich Village in Manhattan. He never left his house during the day, fearing that the FBI would sneak in and plant a bug. At night, he would sneak away from his house and conduct family business when FBI surveillance was more lax. Even then, he only whispered to keep from being picked up by wiretaps.

To avoid incrimination from undercover surveillance, Gigante decreed that any mobster who spoke his name would face severe punishment. In the case of his own family, anyone who spoke his name would be killed on the spot. When necessary, mobsters would either point to their chins or make a "C" with thumb and forefinger when referring to him. In this way, Gigante managed to stay on the streets while the city's other four bosses ended up getting long prison terms.

Another evasive measure Gigante used from 1992 onward was a reformed "administration" structure. Former Salerno protégé Vincent Cafaro had turned informer and identified Gigante as the real boss to the FBI shortly after the Commission Trial, so the use of front bosses no longer protected him. In addition, Gigante was unnerved by Salerno's conviction and long sentence, and decided he needed greater protection. To that end, Gigante instituted two new posts, the "street boss" and the "messenger." The street boss publicly ran the family operations on a daily basis, under Gigante's remote direction. The messenger delivered Gigante's instructions to his capos and soldiers. As a result of these changes, Gigante did not directly communicate with other family mobsters, with the exception of his sons, Vincent Esposito and Andrew Gigante, and a few other close associates.

While the public and media were watching Gigante, other family leaders were running the day-to-day operations of the family. Underboss Venero "Benny Eggs" Mangano operated out of Brooklyn and ran the family's Windows Case rackets. Consigliere Louis "Bobby" Manna, who operated out of the New Jersey faction of the family, as well as supervising four captains around that area during the 1980s.

In 1985, Gigante and other family bosses were shocked and enraged by the murder of Paul Castellano, the Gambino family boss. An ambitious Gambino capo, John Gotti, had capitalized on discontent in that family to murder Castellano and his underboss outside a Manhattan restaurant and become the new Gambino boss. Gotti had violated Cosa Nostra protocol by failing to obtain prior approval for the murder from The Commission. As mentioned above, Gigante had been the triggerman on the last unsanctioned hit on a boss—the hit on Costello. With Castellano dead, Gigante now controlled the Commission and he decided to kill Gotti. Gigante and Lucchese crime family boss Vittorio "Vic" Amuso and underboss Anthony "Gaspipe" Casso hatched a scheme to kill Gotti with a car bomb. On April 13, 1986, a bomb exploded in Gambino underboss Frank DeCicco's car, killing DeCicco. However, Gotti was not in DiCicco's car that day and escaped harm. Although Gigante eventually made peace with Gotti, he remained the most powerful boss in New York. The Genovese family dominated construction and union rackets, gambling rackets, and operations at the Fulton Fish Market and the waterfront operations. During this period, Gigante used intimidation and murder to maintain control of the family.

During the early 1990s, law enforcement used several high profile government informants and witnesses to finally put Gigante in prison. Faced with criminal prosecution, in 1992 Gambino underboss Salvatore "Sammy the Bull" Gravano agreed to testify against Gotti and other Cosa Nostra leaders, including Gigante. Philadelphia crime family underboss Phil Leonetti also became a government witness and testified that during the 1980s, Gigante had ordered the murders of several Philadelphia associates. Finally, Lucchese underboss Anthony Casso implicated Gigante in the 1986 plan to kill John Gotti, Frank DeCicco and

Eugene "Gene" Gotti. While in prison, Gigante was recorded as saying that he'd feigned insanity for 40 years. In 1997, Gigante was convicted on racketeering and conspiracy charges and sentenced to 12 years in federal prison. While Gigante was in prison, the Genovese family was run by acting boss Matthew "Matty the Horse" Ianniello, he received help from capos Ernest Muscarella, Dominick Cirillo, and Gigante's brother Mario. On December 19, 2005, Gigante died in prison from heart disease.

Since the 1990s, infamous mobsters in top positions of the other Five Families of NYC have become informants and testified against many mobsters, putting bosses, capos, and soldiers into prison. The most prominent government witness was Bonanno crime family Boss Joseph "Big Joe" Massino, who started cooperating in 2005. Genovese Underboss Venero "Benny Eggs" Mangano, Consigliere Louis "Bobby" Manna, capo James Ida ("Little Jimmy") and street boss Liborio "Barney" Bellomo received lengthy prison sentences on murder, racketeering and conspiracy convictions. During the last decades, US law enforcement systematically broke down the Genovese crime family, as well as the other Mafia families. Despite these indictments the Genovese family remains a formidable power with approximately 250 made men and 14 active crews as of 2005, according to Selwyn Raab.

Current position and leadership

Vincent Gigante had always despised flashy loudmouths within the ranks of the mob, men who flaunted their gangster status. This was one reason why he hated Gambino boss John Gotti who had seized power by killing the boss of his family without proper Commission approval, which was another strike against him in Gigante's estimation. Gigante was so incensed he put a contract on Gottis head, but the hit was never carried out.

Though Gigante disapproved of ostentatious displays of wealth and power, he did not maintain his disheveled image 24/7. When law-enforcement eyes weren't watching, he found ways to enjoy the perks of power. Besides his wife and five children who lived in a large suburban home, Gigante kept a longtime mistress on the Upper East Side whom he would visit late at night.

Under Gigante the Genovese family maintained the usual organized crime rackets with a few new twists. Every September Manhattans Little Italy hosts the grand Feast of San Gennaro with scores of food concessions and arcade games. The highlight of the festival is a parade that features a life-sized statue of the saint festooned with thousands of dollars in donations hoisted on the shoulders of the faithful and walked through the streets. But according to Jan Hoffman writing in the *New York Times*, hundreds of thousands of dollars that had been earmarked for charities were diverted to the crime family including the fluttering dollar bills that the faithful would pin to the saints statue.

While the family continued its longtime control over the Fulton Fish Market, it also sunk its hooks into the construction of New York City's Jacob K. Javits Convention Center, which broke ground in the late 1980s. John Connolly reported in *New York* magazine that one Manhattan federal prosecutor called it a hiring hall for mobsters and former convicts and 35 percent of carpenters who worked at the Javits center convicted felons. Through the 1990s, the I.M. Pei-designed convention center was one of the family's biggest cash cows.

In 1990 Gigante was arrested and charged with 41 racketeering and conspiracy counts. He evaded prosecution for seven years with his insanity act, but finally the court deemed him sane enough to stand trial, and he was convicted in July 1997. Gigante was sentenced to 10 years in prison and fined $1.25 million. After his conviction, U.S. Attorney Zachary Carter said, The lengths that Vincent Gigante was willing to go to conceal his leadership of the Genovese family speaks volumes about his importance as their leader. His loss will be a devastating blow to the family and to organized crime in general.

Family *messagrio* Dominic Quiet Dom Cirillo was promoted to acting boss, but Cirillo suffered a massive heart attack in 1998, and for years it was uncertain exactly who was running the family, which given the ways of the Genovese's, was exactly how they'd want it. In May 2004, journalist Jerry Capeci reported that Chin Gigante's 80-year-old older brother Mario was poised to take over the top slot in the family.

When Vincent Gigante died in late 2005, the leadership went to Genovese capo Daniel "Danny the Lion" Leo, who was apparently running the day-to-day activities of the Genovese crime family by 2006. In 2006, Genovese underboss and former Gigante loyalist, Venero "Benny Eggs" Mangano was released from prison. That same year, former Gigante loyalist and prominent capo Dominick Cirillo was allegedly promoted to consigliere in prison. By 2008, the Genovese family administration was believed to be whole again. In March 2008, Leo was sentenced to five years in prison for loansharking and extortion. Underboss Venero Mangano is reportedly one of the top leaders within the Manhattan faction of the Genovese crime family. Former acting consigliere Lawrence "Little Larry" Dentico was leading the New Jersey faction of the family until convicted of racketeering in 2006. Dentico was released from prison in 2009. In December 2008, one-time Gigante street boss Liborio "Barney" Bellomo was paroled from prison after serving 12 years. What role Bellomo plays in the Genovese hierarchy is open to speculation, but he is likely to have a major say in the running of the family once his tight parole restrictions are over.

A March 2009 article in the *New York Post* claimed Daniel Leo was still acting boss despite his incarceration. It also estimated that the family consists of approximately 270 "made" members. The Genovese family maintains power and influence in New York, New Jersey, Atlantic City and Florida. It is recognized as the most powerful Cosa Nostra family in the United States. Since Gigante's reign, the Genovese family has been so strong and successful because of its continued devotion to secrecy. According to the FBI, many family associates don't know the names of family leaders or even other associates. This information lockdown makes it more difficult for the FBI to gain incriminating information from government informants.

According to the FBI, the Genovese family has not had an official boss since Gigante's death. Law enforcement considers Leo to be the acting boss, Mangano the underboss, and Cirillo the consigliere. The Genovese family is known for placing top Caporegimes in leadership positions to help the administration run the day-to-day activities of the crime family.

In recent years, according to the New Jersey State Commission of Investigation, the Genovese family has moved into more sophisticated crimes such as computer fraud, stock/securities fraud, and healthcare fraud, often partnering with Russian and Cuban organized crime groups.

At present, capos Bellomo, Ernest Muscarella, Cirillo, and Dentico hold the greatest influence within the family and play major roles in its administration. The Manhattan and Bronx factions, the traditional powers in the family, still exercise that control today.

Historical leadership

Boss (official and acting)

1890s–1909 — Giuseppe "the Clutch Hand" Morello — imprisoned

1910–1916 — Nicholas "Nick Morello" Terranova — murdered on September 7, 1916

1916–1920 — Vincenzo "Vincent" Terranova — stepped down becoming underboss

1920–1922 — Giuseppe "the Clutch Hand" Morello — stepped down becoming underboss to Masseria

1922–1931 — Giuseppe "Joe the Boss" Masseria — murdered on April 15, 1931

1931–1946 — Charles "Lucky" Luciano — imprisoned in 1936, deported to Italy in 1946

Acting 1936–1937 — Vito Genovese — fled to Italy in 1937 to avoid murder charge

Acting 1937–1946 — Frank "the Prime Minister" Costello — became official boss after Luciano's deportation

1946–1957 — Frank "the Prime Minister" Costello — resigned in 1957 after assassination attempt

1957–1969 — Vito "Don Vito" Genovese — imprisoned in 1959, died in prison in 1969

Acting 1959–1962 — Anthony "Tony Bender" Strollo — disappeared in 1962

Acting 1962–1965 — Thomas "Tommy Ryan" Eboli — became front boss

Acting 1965–1969 — Philip "Benny Squint" Lombardo — effectively became the official boss

1969–1981 — Philip "Benny Squint" Lombardo — retired in 1981, died of natural causes in 1987

1981–2005 — Vincent "Chin" Gigante — imprisoned in 1997, died in prison in 2005

Acting 1990–1992 — Liborio "Barney" Bellomo — promoted to street boss

Acting 1997–1998 — Dominick "Quiet Dom" Cirillo — suffered heart attack and resigned

Acting 1998–2005 — Matthew "Matty the Horse" Ianniello — resigned when indicted in July 2005

Acting 2005–2008 — Daniel "Danny the Lion" Leo — imprisoned 2008–2013

Street boss (front boss)

The position of "front boss" was created by boss Philip Lombardo in efforts to divert law enforcement attention from himself. The family maintained this "front boss" deception for the next 20 years. Even after government witness Vincent Cafaro exposed this scam in 1988, the Genovese family still found this way of dividing authority useful. In 1992, the family revived the front boss post under the title of "street boss".

1965–1972 — Thomas "Tommy Ryan" Eboli — murdered in 1972

1972–1980 — Frank "Funzi" Tieri — indicted under RICO statutes and resigned, died in 1981

1981–1992 — Anthony "Fat Tony" Salerno — imprisoned in 1987, died in prison in 1992

1992–1996 — Liborio "Barney" Bellomo — imprisoned from 1996–2008

1998–2001 – Frank Serpico – in 2001 was indicted, in 2002 died of cancer

2001–2002 — Ernest Muscarella — indicted in 2002

2002–2006 — Arthur "Artie" Nigro — indicted in 2006

Underboss

(Official and acting)

1903–1909 — Ignazio "the Wolf" Lupo — imprisoned

1910–1916 — Vincenzo "Vincent" Terranova — became boss

1916–1920 — Ciro "The Artichoke King" Terranova — stepped down

1920–1922 — Vincenzo "Vincent" Terranova — murdered on May 8, 1922

1922–1930 — Giuseppe "Peter the Clutch Hand" Morello — murdered on August 15, 1930

1930–1931 — Joseph Catania — murdered on February 3, 1931

1931–1931 — Charles "Lucky" Luciano — became boss April 1931

1931–1936 — Vito Genovese — promoted to *acting boss* in 1936, fled to Italy in 1937

1937–1951 — Guarino "Willie" Moretti — murdered in 1951

1951–1957 — Vito Genovese — second time as underboss

1957–1972 — Gerardo "Jerry" Catena — also boss of the New Jersey faction; jailed from 1970 to 1972.

1972–1974 — Frank "Funzi" Tieri — promoted to front boss in 1974

1974–1975 — Carmine "Little Eli" Zeccardi

1975–1980 — Anthony "Fat Tony" Salerno — promoted to front boss

1980–1981 — Vincent "Chin" Gigante — promoted to official boss

1981–1987 — Saverio "Sammy" Santora — died of natural causes

1987–present — Venero Mangano — imprisoned in 1991, released December 2006

Acting 1990–1997 — Michael "Mickey Dimino" Generoso — imprisoned in 1997

Acting 1997–2003 — Joseph Zito

Acting 2003–2005 — John "Johnny Sausage" Barbato — imprisoned in 2005

Consigliere

(Official and acting)

1931–1937 — Frank Costello — promoted to *acting boss* in 1937

1937–1957 — "Sandino" — mysterious figure mentioned once by Valachi

1957–1972 — Michele "Mike" Miranda — retired in 1972

1972–1975 — Anthony "Fat Tony" Salerno — promoted to underboss in 1975

1975–1978 — Antonio "Buckaloo" Ferro

Acting 1978–1980 — Dominick "Fat Dom" Alongi

1980–1981 — Dominick "Fat Dom" Alongi

1981–1990 — Louis "Bobby" Manna — imprisoned in 1990

Acting 1989–1990 — James "Little Guy" Ida — promoted to official consigliere

1990–1997 — James "Little Guy" Ida — imprisoned in 1997

1997–2008 — Lawrence "Little Larry" Dentico — imprisoned from 2005–2009

2008-Present - Dominick "Quiet Dom" Cirillo

Messaggero

Messaggero – The messaggero (messenger) functions as liaison between crime families. The messenger can reduce the need for sit-downs, or meetings, of the mob hierarchy, and thus limit the public exposure of the bosses.

1957–1969 — Michael "Mike" Genovese — the brother of Vito Genovese.

1997–2002 — Andrew V. Gigante — the son of Vincent Gigante, indicted 2002

2002–2005 — Mario Gigante

Administrative capos

If the official boss dies, goes to prison, or is incapacitated, the family may assemble a ruling committee of capos to help the acting boss, street boss, underboss, and consigliere run the family, and to divert attention from law enforcement.

1997–2001 — (*four-man committee*) — Dominick "Quiet Dom" Cirillo, Lawrence "Little Larry" Dentico, John "Johnny Sausage" Barbato and Alan "Baldie" Longo — in 2001 Longo was indicted

2001–2005 — (*four-man committee*) — Dominick Cirillo, Lawrence Dentico, John Barbato and Anthony "Tico" Antico — in April 2005 all four were indicted

2005–2010 — (*three-man committee*) — Tino "The Greek" Fiumara (died 2010) the other two are unknown.

Current family members

Administration

Boss Unknown

Acting Boss Daniel "Danny the Lion" Leo - belonged to the Purple Gang of East Harlem in the 1970s. In the late 1990s, Leo joined Vincent Gigante's circle of trusted capos. With Gigante's death in 2005, Leo became *acting boss*. In 2008, Leo was sentenced to five years in prison on loansharking and extortion charges. In March 2010, Leo received an additional 18 months in prison on racketeering charges and was fined $1.3 million. Leo is currently in a community corrections facility. He was released on January 25, 2013.

Street Boss Liborio "Barney" Bellomo – became *Street Boss* in 1992. Bellomo served as *acting boss* for Vincent Gigante during the early 1990s. He controls one of the most influential crews in the crime family, the Manhattan East Harlem and Bronx-based 116th Street Crew. Bellomo was impirsoned in 1996, he was released in July 2008.

Underboss Venero "Benny Eggs" Mangano - became underboss in 1986 under boss Vincent Gigante. A Gigante loyalist, Mangano belonged to the West Side Crew. Mangano was sentenced to 15 years in prison for his involvement in the 1991 "Windows Case". He was convicted of extortion and attempting to manipulate the bidding process of window replacements within municipal housing projects. Released from prison in November 2006, Mangano is reportedly still a Manhattan faction leader.

Consigliere Dominick "Quiet Dom" Cirillo - former capo and trusted aide to boss Vincent Gigante. Cirillo belonged to the *West Side Crew* and was known as one of the *Four Doms*; capos Dominick "Baldy Dom" Canterino, Dominick "The Sailor" DiQuarto and Dominick "Fat Dom" Alongi. Cirillo served as Acting Boss from 1997 to 1998, but resigned due to heart problems. In 2003, Cirillo became acting boss, resigned in 2006 due to his imprisonment on loansharking charges. In August 2008, Cirillo was released from prison. Law enforcement believes that Cirillo is still active in the family.

Capos

New York

Bronx faction

Ernest "Ernie" Muscarella – capo of the 116th Street crew. Muscarella served as acting street boss for Vincent Gigante and Dominick Cirillo in 2002 until his racketeering conviction. He was released from prison on December 31, 2007.

Joseph "Joe D" Dente, Jr. – capo operating in the Bronx. In December 2001, Dente and capos Rosario Gangi and Pasquale Parrello were indicted in Manhattan on racketeering charges. Dente was released from prison on April 29, 2009.

Pasquale "Patsy" Parello – capo operating in the Bronx, he owns a restaurant on Arthur Ave. In 2004, Parello was found guilty of loansharking and embezzlement along with capo Rosario Gangi. Parello was released from prison on April 23, 2008.

Manhattan faction

Conrad Ianniello – capo operating in Manhattan, Brooklyn and Queens. On April 18, 2012 Ianniello was indicted along with members of his crew and was charged with illegal gambling and conspiracy. The conspiracy charge dates back to 2008, when Ianniello along with Robert Scalza and Ryan Ellis tried to extort vendors at the annual Feast of San Gennaro in Little Italy. Conrad Ianniello is related to Robert Ianniello, Jr., who is the nephew to

Matthew Ianniello and the owner of Umberto's Clam House.

Rosario "Ross" Gangi – capo operating in Manhattan, Brooklyn, and New Jersey. Gangi was involved in extortion activities at Fulton Fish Market. He was released from prison on August 8, 2008.

John "Johnny Sausage" Barbato – capo and former driver of Venero Mangano, he was involved in labor and construction racketeering with capos from the *Brooklyn faction*. Barbato was imprisoned in 2005 on racketeering and extortion charges, and released in 2008.

James "Jimmy from 8th Street" Messera – capo of the *Little Italy Crew* operating in Manhattan and Brooklyn. In the 1990s, Messera was involved in extorting the Mason Tenders union and was imprisoned on racketeering charges. He was released from prison on December 12, 1995.

Brooklyn faction

Alphonse "Allie Shades" Malangone – capo operating from Brooklyn and Manhattan. Malagone was very powerful in the 1990s, controlling gambling, loansharking, waterfront rackets and extorting the Fulton Fish Market. Malangone also controlled several private sanitation companies in Brooklyn through *Kings County Trade Waste Association* and *Greater New York Waste Paper Association*. Malagone was arrested in 2000 along with several Genovese and Gambino family members for their activities in the private waste industry.

(*In prison*) Anthony "Tico" Antico – capo involved in labor and construction racketeering in Brooklyn and Manhattan. In 2005, Antico and capos John Barbato and Lawrence

Dentico were convicted of extortion charges. In 2007, he was released from prison. On March 6, 2010, Antico was charged with racketeering in connection with the 2008 robbery and murder of Staten Island jeweler Louis Antonelli. He was acquitted of murder charges, but found guilty of racketeering and is currently in prison with a projected release date of June 12, 2018.

Frank "Punchy" Illiano – capo operating in Brooklyn and Staten Island. Illiano was a high-ranking member of the *Gallo crew* in the Colombo crime family before switching to the Genovese family in the mid-1970s.

Charles "Chuckie" Tuzzo – capo operating in Brooklyn and Manhattan. Tuzzo was involved in pump and dump stock schemes with capo Liborio "Barney" Bellomo. Tuzzo and *acting street boss* Ernest Muscarella infiltrated an International Longshoreman's Association (ILA) local in order to extort waterfront companies operating from New York, New Jersey and Florida. On February 2, 2006, Tuzzo was released from prison after serving several years on racketeering and conspiracy charges.

Queens faction

Anthony "Rom" Romanello – capo operating from Corona Avenue in Corona, Queens Romanello took over Anthony Federici's old crew. In January 2012, he pled guilty to illegal gambling after the cooperating witness died from a heart attack before testifying in the case.

New Jersey

Main article: Genovese crime family New Jersey faction

The Genovese crime family is operating in New Jersey with five crews.

(*Acting*) Stephen Depiro – was the last *acting capo* of the "Fiumara crew". Depiro was overseeing the illegal operations in the New Jersey Newark/Elizabeth Seaport before Fiumara's death in 2010. It is unknown if Depiro still holds this position.

Joseph N. LaScala – capo operating from Hudson County waterfronts cities of Bayonne and Jersey City. LaScala had been Angelo Prisco's *acting capo* before he took over the crew. In May 2012, LaScala and other members of his crew were arrested and charged with illegal gambling in Bayonne.

Ludwig "Ninni" Bruschi – capo operating in South Jersey Counties of Ocean, Monmouth, Middlesex, and North Jersey Counties of Hudson, Essex, Passaic and Union. Bruschi was indicted in June 2003 and paroled in April 2010.

Silvio P. DeVita – capo operating in Essex County.

Lawrence "Little Larry" Dentico – capo operating in South Jersey and Philadelphia. Dentico was *acting* consigliere from 2003 through 2005, when he was imprisoned on extortion, loansharking and racketeering charges. He was released from prison on May 12, 2009.

Soldiers

New York

Salvatore "Sammy Meatballs" Aparo – a former acting capo. His son Vincent is also a made member of the Genovese family. In 2000, Aparo, his son Vincent, and Genovese associate Michael D'Urso met with Abraham Weider, the owner an apartment complex in Flatbush, Brooklyn. Weider wanted to get rid of the custodians union (SEIU Local 32B-J) and was willing to pay Aparo $600,000, but Aparo's associate D'Urso was an FBI informant and had recorded the meeting. In October 2002, Aparo was sentenced to five years in federal prison for racketeering. On May 25, 2006, Aparo was released from prison.

Ralph Anthony "the Undertaker" Balsamo (born in 1971) – a soldier operating in the Bronx and Westchester. Balsamo pleaded guilty in 2007 to narcotics trafficking, firearms trafficking, extortion, and union-related fraud he was sentenced to 97 months in prison. He is currently in a halfway house in New York awaiting his final releas on March 9, 2013.

Louis DiNapoli – soldier with his brother Vincent DiNapoli's 116th Street crew.

Vincent "Vinny" DiNapoli – soldier and former capo with the 116th Street Crew. DiNapol is heavily involved in labor racketeering and has reportedly earned millions of dollars from extortion, bid rigging and loansharking rackets. DiNapoli dominated the N.Y.C. District Council of Carpenters and used them to extort other contractors in

New York. DiNapoli's brother, Joseph DiNapoli, is a powerful capo in the Lucchese crime family.

Anthony "Tough Tony" Federici – former capo in the Queens. Federici is the owner of a restaurant in Corona, Queens. In 2004, Federici was honored by Queens Borough President Helen Marshall for his community service. Federici has since passed on his illicit mob activities to Anthony Romanello.

Albert "Kid Blast" Gallo – acting capo of the Illiano crew in the South Brooklyn neighborhoods of Carroll Gardens, Red Hook, and Cobble Hill. Gallo runs gambling and loan sharking operations in Brooklyn, Manhattan and Staten Island. In the mid-1970s, Gallo transferred from the Gallo crew of the Colombo crime family to the Genovese family and became a made member.

John "Little John" Giglio (April 11, 1958) – also known as "Johnny Bull" is a soldier involved in loansharking.

Federico "Fritzy" Giovanelli – soldier who was heavily involved in loansharking, illegal gambling and bookmaking in the Queens/Brooklyn area. Giovanelli was charged with the January 1986 killing of Anthony Venditti, an undercover NYPD detective, but was eventually acquitted. One known soldier in Giovanelli's crew was Frank "Frankie California" Condo. In 2001, Giovanelli worked with soldier Ernest "Junior" Varacalli in a car theft ring.

Alan "Baldie" Longo – former acting capo of the Malangone crew, he was involved in stock fraud and white-collar crimes in Manhattan and Brooklyn. He was imprisoned on loansharking and racketeering charges, sentenced to 11 years, released in June 2010.

Joseph Olivieri – soldier, operating in the *116th Street Crew* under Capo Louis Moscatiello. Olivieri has been involved in extorting carpenters unions and is tied to labor racketeer Vincent DiNapoli. He was convicted of perjury and was released from Philadelphia CCM on January 13, 2011.

Daniel "Danny" Pagano – former acting capo of the Westchester County–Rockland County crew. Pagano was involved in the 1980s bootleg gasoline scheme with Russian mobsters. In 2007, Pagano was released after serving 105 months in prison.

Ciro Perrone – a former capo. In 1998, Perrone was promoted to captain taking over Matthew Ianniello's old crew. In July 2005, Perrone along with Ianniello and other members of his crew were indicted on extortion, loansharking, labor racketeering and illegal gambling. In 2008, Perrone was sentenced to five years for racketeering and loan sharking. Perrone ran his crew from a social club and Don Peppe's restaurant in Ozone Park, Queens. In 2009, Perrone lost his retrial and was sentenced to five years for racketeering and loan sharking. Perrone was released from prison on October 14, 2011. Perrone died in 2011.

Charles Salzano – a soldier released from prison in 2009 after serving 37 months on loan sharking charges.

Joseph Zito – soldier in the Manhattan faction (*the West Side Crew*) under capo Rosario Gangi. Zito was involved in bookmaking and loansharking business. Law enforcement labeled Zito as acting underboss from 1997 through 2003, but he was probably just a top lieutenant under official underboss Venero "Benny Eggs" Mangano. In the mid-1990s, Zito frequently visited Mangano in prison after his conviction in the Windows Case. Zito relayed messages from Mangano to the rest of the family leadership.

Daniel Cilenti – former soldier in the Brooklyn faction. Inducted into family in 1947, died awaiting trial in March 2012.

New Jersey

Anthony "Tony D." Palumbo – is a former acting capo in the New Jersey faction. Palumbo was promoted *acting boss* of the New Jersey faction by close ally and *acting boss* Daniel "Danny the Lion" Leo. In 2009, Palumbo was arrested and charged with racketeering and murder along Daniel Leo and others. In August 2010 Palumbo pleaded guilty to conspiracy murder charges. He was sentenced to 10 years in prison and his projected release date is November 22, 2019.

Other territories

The Genovese family operates primarily in the New York City area; their main rackets are illegal gambling and labor racketeering.

New York City - The Genovese family operates in all five boroughs of New York as well as in Suffolk, Westchester, Rockland, and Orange Counties in the New York suburbs. The family controls many businesses in the construction, trucking and waste hauling industries. It also operates numerous illegal gambling, loansharking, extortion, and insurance rackets. Small Genovese crews or individuals have operated in Albany, Delaware County, and Utica. The Buffalo, Rochester and Utica crime families or factions traditionally controlled these areas. The family also controls gambling in Saratoga Springs.

Connecticut - The Genovese family has long operated trucking and waste hauling rackets in New Haven, Connecticut. In 2006, Genovese acting boss Matthew "Matty the Horse" Ianniello was indicted for trash hauling rackets in New Haven and Westchester County, New York. In 1981, Gustave "Gus" Curcio and his brother were indicted for the murder of Frank Piccolo, a member of the Gambino crime family.

Massachusetts - Springfield, Massachusetts has been a Genovese territory since the family's earliest days. The most influential Genovese leaders from Springfield were Salvatore "Big Nose Sam" Curfari, Francesco "Frankie Skyball" Scibelli, Adolfo "Big Al" Bruno, and Anthony Arillotta (turned informant 2009). In Worcester, Massachusetts, the most influential capos were Frank Iaconi and Carlo Mastrototaro. In Boston, Massachusetts, the New England or Patriarca crime family from Providence, Rhode Island has long dominated the North End of Boston, but has been aligned with the Genovese family since the Prohibition era. In 2010, the FBI convinced Genovese mobsters Anthony Arillotta and Felix L. Tranghese to become government witnesses. They represent only the fourth and fifth Genovese made men to have cooperated with law enforcement. The government used Arillotta and Tranghese to prosecute capo Arthur "Artie" Nigro and his associates for the murder of Adolfo "Big Al" Bruno.

Florida - The family is active in South Florida

Washington - Seattle, Washington Until the mid-2000s Seattle was an "open city" where all Cosa Nostra families operated freely. The Seattle crew had been working with the Russian mob prior to The Genovese family closing in on the lucrative drug trafficking operation far away from law enforcement eyes in NYC. From 2004–2008 the Genovese family partnered up with mob associate Cory "Fat Cory" Petersen a close friend of Genovese Soldier Ralph Anthony "the Undertaker" Balsamo They trafficked large amounts of cocaine, heroin, ecstasy and oxycontin. The network distributed ecstasy and heroin throughout northern California, Oxycontin and Heroin throughout Washington and ecstasy and cocaine in New York and New Jersey In 2008 "Fat Cory" and crew were charged with heroin trafficking, money laundering and racketeering. In 2011 the feds star witness and government informant died of heart failure just before the case underwent trial all charges since have been dismissed with prejudice.

Family crews

116th Street Crew - led by Liborio "Barney" Bellomo (crew operates in Upper Manhattan and the Bronx)

Greenwich Village Crew - (former crew of Vincent Gigante) (crew operates in Greenwich Village in Lower Manhattan)

Broadway Mob - (operated in Manhattan)

Former members

Dominick "Fat Dom" Alongi – former member of Vincent Gigante's Greenwich Village Crew.

Dominick "Dom The Sailor" DiQuarto – former member of Vincent Gigante's Greenwich Village Crew.

Giuseppe Fanaro - was a member of the Morello family, who was involved in the Barrel murder of 1903. In November 1913, Fanaro was murdered by members of the Lomonte and Alfred Mineo's gangs.

Eugene "Charles" Ubriaco - was a member of the Morello family, he lived on East 114th Street. Ubriaco was arrested in June 1915 for carrying a revolver and was released on bail. On September 7, 1916 Ubriaco along with Nicholas Morello meet with the Navy Street gang in Brooklyn and they both were shot to death on Johson Street in Brooklyn.

Government informants and witnesses

Name Rank and Year

Joseph Valachi Soldier (1963)

Vincent Cafaro Soldier (1986)

George Barone Soldier (2003)

John Bologna Associate (2007)

Anthony Arillotta Soldier (2008)

Felix Tranghese Captain (2008)

Renaldi Ruggiero Captain (2012)

In popular culture

In the 1969 novel *The Godfather* by Mario Puzo, the Corleone family may be based on the Genovese family. Just like Corleone family patriarch Vito Corleone, the Genovese family's original founders came from the village of Corleone as were many of its members. The Corleone family also has a strong presence in areas like Little Italy and the Bronx and is described as the most powerful crime family in the country.

The 1971 film *The French Connection* is about smuggling narcotics (heroin) from Marseille, France to New York

City. In the real French Connection, the heroin was shipped from Sicily to France, then to New York City. Top members of the Genovese family, and the others four families in New York controlled the heroin trade in the United States.

In the 1991 film *Mobsters*, Genovese boss Charlie "Lucky" Luciano was played by Christian Slater. Patrick Dempsey played Meyer Lansky, Costas Mandylor played Frank Costello), and Richard Grieco played Bugsy Siegel). The film was about the formation of the Mafia Commission in the United States.

In the 1991 film *Bugsy*, Genovese boss Lucky Luciano was played by actor Bill Graham. Warren Beatty played Bugsy Siegel) and Ben Kingsley played Meyer Lansky.

In the 1999 film *Bonanno: A Godfather's Story*, Genovese boss Charlie "Lucky" Luciano was played by actor Vince Corazza and boss Vito Genovese by Emidio Michetti.

The 2010 to present HBO U.S. television series *Boardwalk Empire* takes place in 1920s Atlantic City, New Jersey. Mobster Charlie "Lucky" Luciano is played by actor Vincent Piazza. Meyer Lansky is played by Anatol Yusef and Bugsy Siegel is played by Michael Zegen.

Lucchese crime family

Blood and Gravy

On the night of February 26, 1930, Gaetano "Tom" Reina, the first boss of what would eventually become known as the Lucchese crime family, shrugged into his overcoat in the foyer of his aunt's home. It was a Wednesday, and Reina spent every Wednesday with his aunt. He always looked forward to her home-style Sicilian cooking, and she never disappointed him. This evening was no exception. The aroma of her "gravy," as the newly arrived immigrants called their marinara sauce in English, lingered throughout the house.

As Reina stood by the door, his aunt touched his cheek and pulled his collar closed around his neck. It was the dead of winter, and she worried about him. The fact that he was forty years old and the leader of a criminal organization that controlled rackets in the Bronx and ice distribution all throughout New York City made no difference to her. He still needed looking after.

She studied his face, looking for signs of illness or worry, but he immediately broke into a big smile and kissed her cheeks, thanking her for dinner and telling her to be well. But he couldn't fool her. She had seen the worry in his expression—it had been there all night—but Reina wasn't about to burden his elderly aunt with his troubles. She was right—something was bothering him, and it had been eating at him for a long time. His boss, Giuseppe Masseria, had become much too demanding. Masseria was the Mafia boss of all of New York, and he ruled with an iron fist, insisted that everyone call him "Joe the Boss." The greedy bastard now wanted an even bigger slice of the pie, and from Reina's point of view it was undeserved.

Joseph Masseria

For months, Reina had been thinking very seriously about switching his allegiance to Masseria's rival, Salvatore Maranzano, a relative newcomer to New York who had arrived in America from Castellammare del Golfo, Sicily, just a few years earlier. Maranzano was now gaining strength and giving Masseria a run for his money. Reina hadn't totally made up his mind yet, but with every fat envelope that passed from his hands to Masseria's arrogant emissaries, he came that much closer to making his decision.

Reina's aunt caressed his cheek with the palm of her hand and startled him out of his simmering anger. He flashed a quick smile to assure her that everything was all right as he reached for the doorknob and bid her goodbye.

Charles "Lucky" Luciano

As Reina walked down the front steps toward the sidewalk, he noticed a familiar face. Vito Genovese, then 33, who would later become the namesake of the largest crime family in New York, stood under a streetlight, waiting for him. At the time, Genovese was an associate of Charles "Lucky" Luciano, who was "Joe the Boss" Masseria's top lieutenant. Reina started to wave to Genovese, but "as he did," Carl Sifakis writes in *The Mafia Encyclopedia*, "Vito blew his head off." Genovese left Reina's body where it fell, in front of his aunt's house on Sheridan Avenue.

Vito Genovese

Tom Reina became the first victim in the bloody struggle for control of the Sicilian Mafia in America called the Castellammarese War, named after the town in Sicily where many of the participants were born. *But why kill Reina?* many people wondered. Lucky Luciano had been chafing under Masseria's harsh grip himself, and he knew that Reina was thinking about joining forces with the newcomer Maranzano. Why rub out someone who could have been a powerful ally in ousting "Joe the Boss"?

The ingenious Luciano had his reasons.

The Lucchese crime family originated in the early 1920s with Gaetano Reina serving as boss up until his murder in 1930. It was taken over by Tommy Gagliano during the Castellammarese War, and led by him until his death in 1951. The family under Gagliano was peaceful and low key, concentrating their criminal actives in the Bronx, Manhattan and New Jersey. The next boss was Tommy

Lucchese, who turned the family around to become one of the most powerful families to sit on the Commission. Lucchese teamed up with Gambino crime family boss Carlo Gambino to control organized crime in New York City. When Lucchese died of natural causes in 1967, Carmine Tramunti controlled the family for a brief time; he was arrested in 1973. Anthony Corallo then gained control of the family. Corallo was very secretive and soon became one of the most powerful members of the Commission. He was arrested and tried in the famous Commission case of 1986.

For most of its history, the Lucchese family was reckoned as one of the most peaceful crime families in the nation. However, that changed when Corallo decided to put Victor Amuso in charge of the family. Amuso later promoted one of his longtime partners, Anthony Casso to underboss. They instituted one of the bloodiest reigns in Mafia history, ordering virtually anyone who crossed them to be murdered. Amuso was arrested in 1991 and sentenced to life in prison. Several Lucchese wiseguys, fearing for their lives, turned informant. The highest-profile of these was acting boss Alphonse D'Arco, who became the first boss of a New York crime family to testify against the mob. This led to the arrest of the entire Lucchese family hierarchy, with Casso also becoming an informant. Testimony from these informants nearly destroyed the family, though Amuso continued to rule from prison. The current official boss is Steven Crea.

Early history

The early history of the Lucchese crime family can be traced to members of the Morello gang based in East Harlem and the Bronx. Gaetano "Tommy" Reina would leave the Morello's around the time of World War I and created his own family based in East Harlem and the Bronx. As the family's leader, Reina avoided the Mafia-Cammora War for control over New York City. He instead focused on controlling the home ice distribution business throughout New York City. During the early 1920s, Reina became a powerful prohibition era boss and aligned himself with Joseph Masseria, the most powerful Italian-American crime boss in New York. Masseria soon became involved in the Castellammarese War, a vicious gang war with rival *Sicilian boss* Salvatore Maranzano. At this point, Masseria started demanding a share of Reina's criminal profits, prompting Reina to consider changing allegiance to Maranzano. When Masseria learned of Reina's possible betrayal, he plotted with Reina lieutenant Tommy Gagliano to kill him. On February 26, 1930, gunman Vito Genovese murdered Reina outside his aunt's apartment. With Reina dead, Masseria bypassed Gagliano, who expected to take control of the Reina gang, and installed his underling Joseph "Fat Joe" Pinzolo as boss. Furious with this betrayal, Gagliano and Tommy Lucchese secretly defected to Maranzano. In September 1930, Lucchese lured Pinzolo to a Manhattan office building, where Pinzolo was murdered.

The Two Tommies

With Masseria's murder in early 1931, Maranzano won the Castellammarese War. He then outlined a peace plan to all the Sicilian and Italian Mafia leaders in the United States. There would be 24 organizations (to be known as "families") throughout the country that would elect their own *bosses*. Maranzano also reorganized all the Italian-American gangs in New York City into five New York families to be headed by Maranzano, Lucky Luciano, Vincent Mangano, Tommy Gagliano and Joseph Profaci. Gagliano was awarded the old Reina organization, with Lucchese as his underboss and Stefano Rondelli as his consigliere. The final element of Maranzano's peace plan was that he would become the supreme leader of all the families, the *Boss of all Bosses*. However, Luciano and other mob members did not want another top leader. When Maranzano learned about Luciano's disaffection, he hired a gunman to kill him. However, in September 1931 Luciano struck first. Several Jewish assassins provided by Luciano associate Meyer Lansky murdered Maranzano in his office. Luciano now became the most powerful mobster in New York.

Luciano kept the family structure as created by Maranzano, but removed the *Boss of Bosses* in favor of a ruling body, The Commission. The Commission's responsibility was to regulate the families' affairs and resolve all differences between the families. The first Commission members included Luciano family boss Luciano as head of the Commission, Mangano family boss Vincent Mangano, *Gagliano family* boss Tommy Gagliano, Profaci family boss Joseph Profaci, Chicago Outfit boss Al "Scarface" Capone, and Bonanno family boss Joseph Bonanno. Although the Commission was technically a democratic institution, it was actually controlled by Luciano and his allies.

During the 1930s and 1940s, Gagliano and Lucchese led their family into profitable areas of the trucking and clothing industries. When Luciano was sent to prison for pandering in 1936, a rival alliance took control of the Commission. The alliance of Mangano, Bonanno, Buffalo crime family boss Stefano Magaddino, and Profaci used their power to control organized crime in America. Understanding his vulnerability, Gagliano was careful to avoid opposing this new alliance. Gagliano was a quiet man who avoided the media and stayed off the streets. He preferred to pass his orders to the family though Lucchese and a few other close allies. In contrast, Lucchese was the public face of the family who carried out Gagliano's orders. In 1946, Lucchese attended the Cosa Nostra Havana Conference in Cuba on behalf of Gagliano. Gagliano remained the hidden boss of the family until his death in 1953.

"Three-Finger Brown"

Tommy Lucchese was an anomaly among his peers. Five-foot-two with a slight build, he was no stranger to violence. As Carl Sifakis points out, he may have been Lucky Luciano's "favorite killer," and may have also been involved in some 30 murders. This would have been high praise coming from Luciano, who at one time had Albert "Lord High Executioner" Anastasia, among other heavy hitters, in his stable. Lucchese lost a finger in 1915, which earned him the nickname "Three-Finger Brown" after a popular baseball player at the time. As a young man, he racked up a long list of arrests, including ones for homicide, but he managed to avoid conviction in every case except for a single grand larceny charge in the early 1920s.

Lucchese had served loyally as underboss to Tom Gagliano for 22 years. Like Gagliano, he set ego aside and concentrated on core Mafia values—making money and not getting caught. Having lived under the tyrannical reigns of the "Mustache Petes," Lucchese showed more care for the welfare of his men when it was his turn to become boss. Popular and well-liked by his soldiers, he took his family into new rackets in Manhattan's garment district and in the related trucking industry. According to mob expert Jerry Capeci, Lucchese's successful infiltration into these businesses would indicate his control over "key Teamsters and Ladies Garment Workers locals as well as trade associations."

Lucchese was a modern gangster in the Luciano mold who branched out into new areas while maintaining the bread-and-butter rackets that have always been the foundation of the Mafia's money-making machine—gambling, construction, loan-sharking, and drugs. Along with

Gagliano, he pioneered   rackets at the newly opened
Idelwild Airport (later renamed Kennedy Airport),
corrupting unions there to facilitate trucking monopolies,
warehouse theft, and hijacking.

But Lucchese also had a talent for making friends in high
places and using those friendships to his advantage.
Among his good friends was Armand Chankalian,
administrative assistant to the United States Attorney of the
Southern District of New York. Chankalian introduced him
to U.S. Attorney Myles Lane. In 1945, Lucchese applied to
the New York State Parole Board for a certificate of good
conduct, and Chankalian served as a character witness for
him.   The certificate was granted.

Thomas Murphy

Lucchese also counted Assistant U.S. Attorney Thomas
Murphy among his friends. Murphy is best known for
prosecuting accused Communist spy Alger Hiss for perjury

in 1949.   Murphy was named police commissioner of the city of New York when Mayor Vincent Impellitteri won re-election in 1950. Tommy Lucchese was among Impellitteri's staunchest supporters and had been a frequent guest at Murphy's home. The commissioner claimed total ignorance of Lucchese's criminal record until that year.

Lucchese era

After Gagliano's death in 1951, Lucchese became family boss and appointed Vincenzo Rao as his Consigliere and Stefano LaSalle as his Underboss. Lucchese continued with Gagliano's policies, making the now Lucchese family one of the most profitable in New York. Lucchese established control over Teamsters union locals, workers' co-operatives and trade associations, and rackets at the new Idlewild Airport. Lucchese also expanded family rackets in Manhattan's Garment District and in related trucking industry around New York City. Lucchese built close relations with many powerful New York politicians, including Mayors William O'Dwyer and Vincent Impellitteri and members of the judiciary, who aided the family on numerous occasions. Throughout his regime, Lucchese kept a low profile and saw to it that his men were well taken care of.

When Lucchese became boss, he helped Vito Genovese and Carlo Gambino in their fights to take control of their families. The three plotted to take over the Mafia Commission by murdering family bosses Frank Costello and Albert Anastasia. On May 2, 1957 Costello survived an assassination attempt and immediately decided to retire as boss in favor of Genovese. Then on October 25, 1957, the Gallo brothers (from the Colombo family) murdered Anastasia, allowing Gambino to become boss. Lucchese and Gambino started conspiring to remove their former ally Genovese. After the disastrous 1957 Apalachin meeting of mob leaders in Upstate New York, Genovese lost a great deal of respect in the Commission. In 1959, with the assistance of Luciano, Costello, and Meyer Lansky, Genovese was arrested.

Gambino and Lucchese assumed full control of the Mafia Commission. In 1960, they backed the Gallo brothers in their rebellion against Profaci family boss Joe Profaci. Gambino and Lucchese saw the war as a way to take over rackets from the distracted Profaci's. After uncovering a plot by Joseph Bonanno to assassinate them, Lucchese and Gambino used the Commission to strip Bonanno of his role as boss. This power play started a war within the Bonanno family and served to strengthen both the Lucchese and Gambino families.

As mob bosses go, Lucchese was a worthy namesake for the family he led. He maintained his criminal lifestyle for 44 years without a conviction, a major feat in itself. Toward the end of his life he suffered from heart disease and underwent surgery for a brain tumor, from which he never fully recovered. He died on July 13, 1967. Over 1,000 people attended his funeral, including many high-ranking mobsters who knew that police and FBI surveillance teams would be watching. Tommy Lucchese was so well-respected, nothing would keep them away.

Carmine Trumunti succeeded Lucchese as boss, but his term was relatively short and undistinguished. He was convicted of sanctioning narcotics trafficking and sentenced to life in prison. The next boss followed more closely in the footsteps of "Three-Finger Brown."

Tramunti and the French Connection

At the time of his appointment as temporary boss, Carmine "Mr. Gribbs" Tramunti was in ill health. With boss-in-waiting Anthony "Tony Ducks" Corallo in prison, Tramunti was expected to hold power until Corallo's release. Tramunti faced a number of criminal charges during his time as acting boss and was eventually convicted of financing a large heroin smuggling operation, the infamous French Connection. This scheme was responsible for distributing millions of dollars in heroin along the East Coast during the early seventies.

Before the French Connection trial, the seized heroin was stored in the NYPD property/evidence storage room pending trial. In a brazen scheme, criminals stole hundreds of kilograms of heroin worth $70 million from the room and replaced them with bags of flour. Officers discovered the theft when they noticed insects eating the so-called heroin. The scope and depth of this scheme is still unknown, but officials suspect the thieves had assistance from corrupt NYPD officers. Certain plotters received jail sentences, including Vincent Papa (he was later assassinated in the Atlanta Federal Penitentiary in Atlanta, Georgia). In 1974, after Tramunti's incarceration, Corallo finally took charge of the family.

Corallo and the Jaguar

FBI mugshot of Anthony Corallo

After Tramunti's incarceration in 1974, Anthony Corallo finally took control of the Lucchese family. Corallo came from the Queens faction of the family. Known as "Tony Ducks" from his ease at 'ducking' criminal convictions, Corallo was a boss squarely in Lucchese's mold. By the 1950s, Corallo was one of several mobsters who had a tight grip over union locals with the tacit sanction of union officials. Corallo's cash cow was Teamsters Local 239 in New York. He was accused of creating dummy employees and pocketing their salaries, which amounted to $69,000 by the time authorities learned of this scam. Corallo and other mobsters worked hand-in-hand with Jimmy Hoffa, international Teamsters president, who had no problem with wiseguys looting union funds as long as they made sure the locals they controlled kept him in power. Corallo was cited by the U.S. Senate Labor Rackets Committee (better known as the McClellan Committee) as a major player in union corruption. Robert Kennedy, the committee's chief counsel, appeared on a nationally broadcast late-night television talk show to denounce

Corallo and other mobsters by name. Subpoenaed to testify before the committee, Corallo was unflappable, invoking his Fifth Amendment rights 83 times when questioned about a bugged conversation in which Jimmy Hoffa seemed to be giving his blessings to Corallo's illegal union activities.

Corallo appointed Salvatore "Tom Mix" Santoro as the Underboss and supervisor of all labor and construction racketeering operations in New York, and Christopher "Christie Tick" Furnari as the reputed Consigliere. The family prospered under Corallo's leadership, particularly in narcotics trafficking, labor racketeering, and major illegal gambling.

Salvatore Avellino Jr.

"Tony Ducks" managed to duck trouble with the union investigations, but he did get snagged for bribing a New York Supreme Court justice and an assistant U.S. attorney and served a two-year stretch as a result.

Years later he was convicted on charges of bribing the New York City Water Commissioner, James L. Marcus, in an attempt to get contracts to clean and repair parts of the city's reservoir system. The contracts were worth over $800,000, and Corallo was sentenced to four and a half years in prison.

Carmine Trumunti

By the time Corallo was released, Tommy Lucchese was on his deathbed and Carmine Trumunti was waiting in the wings. A few years later Trumunti was sent away to prison, and the family was in sore need of a stabilizing force, which Corallo provided for twelve years. Under Corallo's leadership, the Lucchese Family, though smaller in number than the Genovese and Gambino families, prospered and grew. In narcotics trafficking alone, they profited handsomely when a family associate named Matty Madonna became the main supplier for Leroy Nicky

Barnes, the heroin king of Harlem. Madonna sold Barnes up to 40 kilos a month in the heady disco days of the early 1970s. The family's rackets ran smoothly and stealthily for many years, until Tony Ducks was bitten by a Jaguar.

Corallo never discussed business during sit-downs, fearing that the FBI was monitoring the conversations. Instead, he used the car phone in the Jaguar owned by his bodyguard and chauffeur's. Corallo was driven around New York while on the phone discussing business. Salvatore "Sal" Avellino and Aniello "Neil" Migliore shifted as Corallo's chauffeurs during the 1970s and 1980s.

Corallo, a huge fan of the New Jersey faction of the family, reputedly inducted and promoted Anthony "Tumac" Accetturo and Michael "Mad Dog" Taccetta into the organization and put them in charge of the Jersey Crew, which reportedly controlled most of the loansharking and illegal gambling operations in Newark, New Jersey at the time.

In the early 1980s, the Federal Bureau of Investigation (FBI) finally managed to plant a bug in the Jaguar. The FBI recorded Corallo speaking at great length about mob affairs, including illegal gambling, labor racketeering, drug trafficking, and murder. Corallo was arrested and put on trial along with all the heads of the Five Families at the time. This trial became legendary as the Mafia Commission Trial. Backed up by the RICO statutes, the government went after the heads of the New York families, attempting to prove that these men controlled an ongoing criminal enterprise. In 1986, Corallo was found guilty and sent to prison, where he died in 2000.

Corallo handpicked his own successor, and like other bosses before him, he picked the wrong man. (If Carlo

Gambino had chosen his popular underboss, Aniello Dellacroce, to succeed him instead of his brother-in-law, Paul Castellano, John Gotti might never have become the Dapper Don.) Corallo's choice was Vittorio "Vic" Amuso, a man who in a former life might have operated the guillotine during the French Revolution.

On December 16, 1985, Gambino crime family boss Paul Castellano was murdered without Commission approval. The Genovese and Lucchese family teamed up and plotted John Gotti's murder. The alliance had Gambino underboss Frank DeCicco murdered but failed its attempts to kill Gotti.

On January 13, 1987 Corallo was convicted on numerous charges and was sentenced to 100 years in prison, where he died in 2000. To succeed him as boss, Corallo originally chose acting boss Anthony "Buddy" Luongo. However, Luongo disappeared in 1986. Corallo's ultimate choice was Vittorio "Vic" Amuso. Allegedly both Amuso and Anthony "Gaspipe " Casso were candidates for the job. Evidence suggests that Corallo wanted Casso, but Casso convinced him to select Amuso instead. Amuso made Casso his underboss in 1989, allowing him to exert great influence over family decisions.

The iron fists of

Amuso and Casso

FBI surveillance photo of Casso (right) with Lucchese
family boss, Vittorio Amuso

During the late 1980s, the Lucchese family underwent a
period of great turmoil. Vittorio "Vic" Amuso and his
fierce underboss, Anthony "Gaspipe" Casso, instituted one
of the most violent reigns in American Mafia history. Both
men were heavily involved in labor racketeering, extortion,
drug trafficking and committed many murders. Amuso and
Casso were strong rivals of Gambino crime family boss
John Gotti and strong allies of Genovese crime family boss
Vincent "Chin" Gigante. Angry over Gotti's unauthorized
murder of Gambino boss Paul Castellano, Amuso, Casso,
and Gigante conspired to murder Gotti. On April 13, 1986 a
car-bombing killed Gambino underboss Frank DeCicco,
but missed Gotti. This assassination attempt sparked a long

and confusing 'tension' between these three crime families with many deaths reported on all sides.

Anthony "Tumac" Accetturo

During the late 1980s, Amuso began demanding 50% of the profits generated by the Jersey Crew. New Jersey leaders Anthony Accetturo and Michael Taccetta refused Amuso's demand. In retaliation, Amuso and Casso ordered the entire New Jersey faction of the Lucchese family killed, 30 members in all —the now-infamous "whack Jersey" order. Disillusioned with Amuso's haphazard leadership, New Jersey boss Anthony "Tumac" Accetturo had stopped giving the New York leadership a piece of his pie. From Accetturo's point of view, the members of the Jersey faction were hard-working moneymakers who got nothing but trouble from the New York bosses. All this killing and shooting was bringing the heat down on the Lucchese family members and was bad for business. Accetturo tried negotiating with Amuso and Casso, but there was no placating them. The order stood. "Whack New Jersey!" He summoned them to a meeting in Brooklyn. Fearful for their lives, all the Jersey crew members skipped the meeting and went into hiding.

Taccetta and Accetturo were later put on trial in 1990, as both Amuso and Casso were implicated in a case involving the fitting of thousands of windows in New York at over-inflated prices, and the pair went into hiding of that same year, naming Alphonse "Little Al" D'Arco as acting boss. For the next few years, Amuso and Casso ruled the family from afar and ordered the execution of anyone they deemed troublesome, either they were considered rivals or potential informants. All of this convinced many Lucchese wiseguys that Amuso and Casso were no longer acting or thinking rationally.

Alphonse D'Arco in a 1970s FBI surveillance photo

What followed next was a series of botched hits on family members suspected of being informants. Ironically, these hits caused several family members to actually turn informer. Amuso ordered the slaying of capo Peter "Fat Pete" Chiodo, who along with Casso was in charge of the *Windows Case* operation. He was shot 12 times, but still survived. After Amuso ordered hits on Chiodo's wife and sister in violation of longstanding rules against women being harmed, Chiodo turned state's evidence and provided the entire windows operation that eventually controlled $150 million in window replacements, sold in New York City. As Amuso also sanctioned the hit on Anthony Accetturo, who was on trial in 1990, he also cooperated with the government.

Anthony Casso

At this point, acting boss "Little Al" D'Arco must have thought he'd fallen down the rabbit hole and landed at the Mad Hatter's tea party. Amuso and Casso were getting more unreasonable and making less sense. As author Ernest Volkman writes in his book *Gangbusters,* at a clandestine meeting, Casso gave D'Arco a list of 49 names -- people Casso had slated for execution. D'Arco scanned down the list and realized that half of these people were Lucchese members. When D'Arco questioned some of Casso's choices, the underboss said they all had to be killed because they were "creeps." According to Volkman, at another meeting Casso promised that he would throw a party when he finally came out of hiding and invite all the "creeps" so he could kill them all in one place.

The planned executions went as high as acting boss D'Arco. Furious over the failed hit on Chiodo, Amuso set up D'Arco to be killed at a Manhattan hotel. However, this hit also came undone after D'Arco saw a man hide a gun in his shirt, then slip it into the bathroom. Recognizing this as a classic setup for a hit, D'Arco fled for his life and turned himself over to the authorities to spare him and his family from Amuso and Casso and their increasingly erratic demands. He was the first boss of a New York crime family, acting or otherwise, to become an informant.

John Gotti

Amuso showed his megalomania when he ordered D'Arco to recruit a bomb expert from the Philadelphia Mafia family, who would rig an explosive that would kill Gambino boss John Gotti. D'Arco pointed out that there would most certainly be retaliation from the Gambino family, and the Lucchese family didn't need any more trouble. Amuso told him not to worry about it because "the robe," Genovese boss Vincent Gigante, would support them.

These two were out of control, D'Arco must have thought. If they could order the deaths of their own family members and their loved ones, how safe was he? The writing on the wall came when Amuso demoted him and made him one of a four-man committee appointed to run the family. He knew that Amuso and Casso held him responsible for the botched hit on "Fat Pete" Chiodo. "Little Al" decided he'd better start watching his back more than usual.

Six weeks later, D'Arco walked into the Hotel Kimberly in midtown Manhattan and took the elevator up to a suite where the acting Lucchese hierarchy had planned to hold a meeting. As soon as he stepped into the suite, he knew instinctively that something was wrong. According to Alan May, "D'Arco noticed one of the men had a bulge under his shirt, a sure sign he was carrying a weapon." Coming armed to a meeting was a clear violation of Mafia protocol. The man with the bulge excused himself and went into the bathroom. When he returned, the bulge was gone. D'Arco's stomach sank. It was a classic setup. The next guy to go into the john would come out with the gun in his hand.

"Little Al" was certain that he was their target. He had to be, he thought. He tried to think of a way he could escape, but he was outnumbered. He'd never even make it to the door.

When another man went into the bathroom, D'Arco was convinced his number was up. But when the man came out, nothing happened. He probably wasn't the designated shooter, D'Arco figured. Maybe he just had to go pee. The shooter had yet to make his move.

That's when D'Arco decided he had to get the hell out of there. He made a quick excuse and left the suite, hightailing it to the lobby and out onto the street. He scanned the block outside the hotel but couldn't find his driver, a sure sign that he'd been marked for execution that day. He quickly flagged down a cab and went directly to his home, where he gathered up his wife and family. They immediately fled for their lives.

D'Arco felt betrayed. He had lived his life by the Mafia code and had been 100% loyal to the Lucchese family, but the rules set down by the godfathers of previous generations didn't mean anything anymore. Amuso and Casso had gone off the reservation, not him. It shamed him to be running away, because he hadn't done anything wrong. His first thought wasn't to run into the arms of the law, but with a wife and a big family to protect (particularly his son Joseph, who had been part of the hit team that failed to kill "Fat Pete" Chiodo), and no one in the mob willing to help them, D'Arco had little choice.

"Little Al" D'Arco became the first Mafia boss in history to turn state's witness and testify against his fellow family members after the government agreed to put him and his extended family in witness protection. He wouldn't be the last.

Law enforcement eventually caught up with the two fugitives. On July 29, 1991, the FBI captured Amuso and his bodyguard at a suburban mall near Scranton, Pennsylvania, and on January 19, 1993 the FBI captured Casso in Mount Olive, New Jersey. Amuso steadfastly refused all offers from the government to make a deal and become a government witness. In contrast, Casso quickly agreed to a deal on March 1, 1994 and started revealing family secrets. One of the biggest secrets was that Casso had been paying two New York Police Department detectives, Louis Eppolito and Stephen Caracappa, to provide Casso with sensitive police information and even perform to contract murders. Casso related how Eppolito and Caracappa, on Christmas Day 1986, murdered an innocent Brooklyn man who had the same name as a suspected government informant. Casso told the government that in 1992 Lucchese hit men tried to kill the sister of another suspected informant, violating the alleged Mafia "rule" barring violence against family members. However, in 1998, prosecutors tore up the deal after accusing Casso of lying about other mob turncoats and bribing guards, among other things. As a result, the court ordered no leniency for Casso at his sentencing, and he was sentenced to 13 consecutive terms of life in prison.

In January 1993, Amuso received a life sentence. In 1994, Casso also received a life sentence. Casso had reportedly conspired with reputed consigliere Frank Lastorino and Brooklyn faction leaders George Zappola, George Conte, Frank "Bones" Papagni and Frank Gioia, Jr. into murdering Steven "Wonderboy" Crea, Amuso's acting underboss of the Bronx, as well as Gambino crime family acting boss John "Junior" Gotti, son of the imprisoned John Gotti, along with members of the Genovese crime family once again. But due to massive indictments, none of the plots were committed.

The Gaspipe Backfires

Frank DeCicco

In 1993, Anthony "Gaspipe" Casso was finally caught. He'd been on the lam for 30 months, staying with an old girlfriend in central New Jersey. The government couldn't wait to get him into court. Having allegedly participated in 36 murders, including the bombing of Gambino underboss Frank DeCicco in 1986 and a plot to rub out federal Judge Eugene Nickerson, Casso would be easy pickings. In all likelihood, they'd be able to lock him away for the rest of his life. But Casso, unlike his boss Vic Amuso, decided there was nothing to be gained from being a standup guy. Instead, he flipped, offering to testify against the mob.

Sammy "the Bull" Gravano

It was a surprise move, but not an unwelcome one.
Government prosecutors knew he was a treasure chest of
inside information, not only about the Lucchese family, but
about some of the other families, and they compared him to
another valuable turncoat, Gambino underboss Sammy
"Bull" Gravano, whose testimony against Gambino boss
John Gotti helped put away the elusive Teflon Don.   But
Casso apparently didn't understand that turncoats are
supposed to show that they've turned a corner in their lives
and want to leave their criminal ways behind them. If
anything, Gaspipe seemed to feel that cooperating with the
government gave him license to misbehave.

DeCiccos bombed out car

Incarcerated in a special prison unit for cooperating witnesses, Casso frequently picked fights with other inmates. In one instance, he assaulted a handcuffed prisoner in the shower room. On another occasion, he attacked an inmate twice his size with a rolled-up magazine. The 350-pound prisoner grabbed the 165-pound Casso by the shirtfront and beat him mercilessly until guards tore them apart. Both men were relegated to solitary confinement as a result.

Anthony Casso in jail

Jerry Capeci writes in his article "Gaspipes Gets Gassed" that Casso also sweet-talked a prison secretary into doing favors for him, including giving him use of an unmonitored telephone. Casso also "bribed guards at the Otisville Correctional Facility to supply him with cash, steaks, sushi, turkeys, vodka, wine and other contraband."

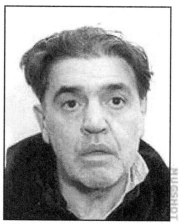
Vincent "the Chin" Gigante

Casso was proving to be a loose cannon, and prosecutors feared what he would do on the stand if he were ever used as a witness. They decided not to use him in the trial against Genovese boss, Vincent "Chin" Gigante, relying instead on the testimonies of Sammy Gravano and "Little Al" D'Arco. Casso was so incensed that he'd been passed over, he wrote a letter to federal prosecutors in Brooklyn after Gigante's conviction and blasted the turncoat witnesses, accusing Gravano and D'Arco of lying on the stand. Prosecutors must have blown a gasket when they received his written temper tantrum, fearing that this document could jeopardize their hard-won conviction.

This time, Casso had gone too far. He was booted out of the program and evicted from the witness-protection unit of the prison. Branded a rat by his former mob cohorts, he had to be housed by himself in solitary confinement for his own protection. Prosecutors then wrote their own letter to the court, recommending that Casso not be given leniency in sentencing for cooperation that never paid off. They asked that Casso be given a life sentence, which is exactly what he got. His sushi and steak days were over.

A Revolving Door

Joseph "Little Joe" Defede

In 1993, Vic Amuso, still the boss of the Lucchese family, made his wishes known from behind prison walls. His choice to lead the family as acting boss in his absence was his handball partner from his old Queens neighborhood, Joseph "Little Joe" Defede. After years of turmoil and internal strife, the Lucchese Family seemed to be on an even keel. But then Amuso started checking the books. He found that the family rackets weren't making as much money as they had been, and he suggested that Defede might be skimming off the top of the family's garment district rackets.

In his article "A Lousy Legacy," Jerry Capeci quotes an unnamed source as saying that Defede, who was never known for being a "tough guy," feared that Amuso would have him "whacked" for stealing from the family. After serving nearly five years as acting boss, he turned himself in to the FBI and pleaded guilty to extorting a small fortune from businesses in the garment district. For "Little Joe," who had started his criminal career running a numbers operation out of a hot-dog truck in Brooklyn, it was an easy choice: better to be alive in prison than dead in the street. While lying in a prison hospital bed in Lexington, Kentucky, Defede took a hard look at his life and decided that there was nothing left for him in the mob. He decided to follow "Little Al" D'Arco's lead and turn government witness.

Next up in the top slot was underboss Steven Crea, but his term as acting boss didn't last long. He was soon convicted on state racketeering charges involving the construction industry and sent to prison.

Acting bosses

FBI mugshot of Steven Crea

When Amuso went to prison, he chose Joseph "Little Joe" DeFede to be his acting boss. Throughout the mid-1990s Amuso continued to control the family from prison. DeFede, who supervised the powerful Garment District racket, reportedly earned more than $40,000 to $60,000 a month. DeFede placed Steven Crea in charge of the family's labor and construction racketeering operations. Crea increased the Lucchese family earnings from these rackets between $300,000 and $500,000 every year. But as US law enforcement kept pressuring the organized crime activities in New York, DeFede was arrested and indicted on nine counts of racketeering in 1998. DeFede pled guilty to the charges and was sentenced to five years in prison. Angry at DeFede's guilty plea, Amuso promoted Crea as the new acting boss.

Steven "Wonderboy" Crea success with the labor and construction rackets convinced Amuso that DeFede had been previously skimming off these profits. In late 1999, Amuso placed a *contract* on DeFede's life. On September 6, 2000, Crea and seven other Lucchese members were arrested and jailed on extortion charges, mostly to the supervising of the construction sites with various capos Dominic Truscello and Joseph Civitello.

Louis Diadone

Crea's successor met a similar fate. In September 2004, the Lucchese Family's next acting boss, Louis "Louie Crossbay" Daidone, was convicted in federal court on loansharking and murder charges. "Little Al" D'Arco, testifying for the prosecution, claimed that when he had been acting boss of the Lucchese Family, he had ordered Daidone to kill a man he feared would turn government witness. He said he told Daidone to stuff a canary in the corpse's mouth as a warning to any others who might be thinking about spilling their guts to the government. With the aid of a magnifying glass, jurors were able to spot the canary in the victim's mouth in crime scene photographs, and, as a result, voted to convict Daidone.

It should be noted that the Lucchese Family has inspired some of the most notable mob characters on film and television. The Martin Scorsese film *Goodfellas* is based on Nicholas Pileggi's nonfiction book *Wiseguy*, which follows the life and crimes of Lucchese associate Henry Hill. In that movie, actor Paul Sorvino plays "Paul Cicero," a character modeled on the real-life Lucchese capo Paul Vario. Henry Hill (played by Ray Liotta) and Jimmy "the Gent" Burke (played by Robert DiNiro) were both associates in Vario's crew.

Mafia cops

In April 2006, Casso revealed that two respected New York City police detectives worked as hitmen and informants for Casso during the 1980s and early 1990s before their retirement. They were Louis Eppolito and Stephen Caracappa, who spent much of their combined 44 years with the NYPD committing murders and leaking confidential information to the Lucchese family. Between 1986 and 1990, Eppolito and Caracappa participated in eight murders and received $375,000 from Casso in bribes and payments for murder 'contracts'. Casso used Caracappa and Eppolito to pressure the Gambino crime family by murdering several of their members. This is because Casso, along with the imprisoned Amuso and Genovese crime family boss Vincent Gigante, wanted their rival John Gotti out of the way. Caracappa and Eppolito are now seen as the main source of 'tension' between these three families during the late 1980s and early 1990s.

For one contract, Eppolito and Caracappa kidnapped mobster James Hydell, forced him into their car trunk, and delivered him to Casso for torture and murder. Hydell's body was never found. The two detectives also shot Bruno Facciolo, who was found in Brooklyn in the trunk of a car with a canary in his mouth. After pulling Gambino crime family captain Edward "Eddie" Lino for a routine traffic check, the detectives murdered him on the expressway in his Mercedes-Benz. In 2006, Eppolito and Caracappa were convicted of murdering Hydell, Nicholas Guido, John "Otto" Heidel, John Doe, Anthony DiLapi, Facciolo, Lino, and Bartholomew Boriello on the orders of Casso and the Lucchese family. They were sentenced to life imprisonment.

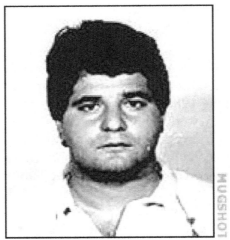

Michael Taccetta

Prosecutors and investigators from New Jersey believe that Michael Taccetta, street boss for the Garden State faction of the Lucchese Family, is the likely inspiration for "Tony Soprano" (played by James Gandolfini), the main character of HBO's *The Sopranos*. They also cite close similarities between Lucchese hitman Tommy Ricciardi and Tony Soprano's *consigliere* "Silvio Dante" (played by Steven Van Zandt). Both Taccetta and Ricciardi were on Vic Amuso's hit list when he decreed that the Jersey faction of the Lucchese Family should be made extinct.

Ruling panel

With the arrest of *acting boss* Louis Daidone in 2003, imprisoned boss Vic Amuso put a three-man ruling panel to run the family. The panel consisted of capos Aniello Migliore, Joseph DiNapoli and Matthew Madonna who brought the family's power back into the Bronx.

On December 18, 2007, two members of the panel Joseph DiNapoli and Matthew Madonna were arrested along with New Jersey faction capo Ralph V. Perna, soldier Nicodemo Scarfo, Jr. and others. The arrested came after New Jersey law enforcement agencies revealed that through investigation *Operation Heat* the New Jersey faction controlled a $2.2 billion illegal gambling, money laundering and racketeering ring from New Jersey to Costa Rica.

On October 1, 2009, the Lucchese family was hit with two separate indictments charging 49 members and associates with bribery and racketeering. In the first indictment 29, members and associates of the Lucchese family were arrested. The indicted charged Joseph DiNapoli, Matthew Madonna and *acting capo* Anthony Croce with running operations that nearly grossed $400 million from illegal gambling, loansharking, gun trafficking, bribery and extortion. In the second indictment obtained from investigation *"Operation Open House"* 12 more Lucchese mobsters were charged with bribery. Acting capo Andrew Disimone and others mobsters were charged with bribing New York Police Department (NYPD) detective and sergeant posing as crooked cops to protect illegal poker parlors.

Current position

Although in prison for life, Victor Amuso remained the official boss of the Lucchese crime family until 2009. Amuso had been boss for almost a quarter-century but it is unclear how much influence he had over the crime family's day-to-day affairs in later years. From 2003-2009, a three-man ruling panel consisting of Aniello "Neil" Migliore, Joseph DiNapoli and Matthew Madonna had been running the family. All three men are long time capos in the family, but Migliore was believed to be the most powerful. Arguably, Migliore, DiNapoli and Madonna brought stability to the Lucchese family during the 2000s. The family's presence remains strong in the Bronx, Manhattan, Queens, and New Jersey.

A February 2004, *New York Post* article stated that, the Lucchese family consisted of about 9 capos and 82 soldiers. In March 2009, an article in the *New York Post* stated that the Lucchese family consisted of approximately 100 "made" members.

In late 2009, the Lucchese family was handed three federal indictments showing that the family continues to be very active in organized crime, especially in labor racketeering, illegal gambling, and extortion. In one of the indicitments ruling panel members Joseph DiNapoli and Matthew Madonna were charged with controlling a ring that extorted and bribed businesses and construction sites in Manhattan and the Bronx. Also in 2009, Steven Crea's parole expired and consigliere Joseph Caridi was released from prison after serving almost six years.

On January 16, 2013, the FBI arrested 29 members and associates of the Genovese, Lucchese and Gambino crime families on racketeering charges related to their involvement in carting companies in Westchester County, Rockland County and Nassau County in New York, and Bergen County and Passaic County in New Jersey. Members and associates of the Genovese, Lucchese and Gambino crime families controlled waste disposal businesses by dictating which companies could pick up trash at certain location and extorting protection payments preventing further extortion from other mobsters.

In June 2013, the New York FBI office reduced the number of agents, focused on investigating the five crime families to thirty-six agents, divided into two squads. In the past the FBI had a separate squad of 10 to 20 agents investigating each crime family. Now the FBI will have "squad C5" which at one time just investigated the Genovese family will also be investigating the Bonanno and Colombo families, while "squad C16" which before just investigated the Gambino family will be also investigating the Lucchese family.

Current family members

Administration

Boss Steven "Wonderboy" Crea: became Underboss in 1993 then acting boss in 1998. On September 6, 2000, Crea along with other Lucchese family members was indicted and charged with extortion and supervising various construction sites in New York City. In January 2004, Crea was sentenced to 34 months in prison. Crea was released from prison on August 24, 2006. Crea became boss in late 2009.

Underboss Unknown

Consigliere Joseph "Joe C." Caridi: operating from Long Island and Queens. Caridi was imprisoned on extortion and loansharking charges and was released on November 27, 2009.

Caporegimes

The Bronx faction

Capo: Joseph "Joey Dee" DiNapoli: served on a *ruling panel* that ran the family from 2003–2009 along with Aniello Migliore and Matthew Madonna. In December 2007, DiNapoli and Madonna were arrested along with members of the New Jersey faction on illegal gambling charges. On October 1, 2009 DiNapoli and Madonna were indicted in a racketeering scheme that involved mob-tied building inspectors and soliciting bribes to overlook violations.

Capo: Matthew "Matt" Madonna: served on a *ruling panel* that ran the family from 2003–2009 along with Aniello Migliore and Joseph DiNapoli. In December 2007, Madonna and DiNapoli were arrested along with members of the New Jersey faction on illegal gambling charges. On October 1, 2009 Madonna and DiNapoli were indicted on racketeering, illegal gambling and bribery charges.

Capo: John "Johnny Hooks" Capra: was indicted in 2005 along with members of the Gambino crime family on extortion and illegal gambling charges. Capra was released from prison on September 10, 2008.

Capo: Anthony "Blue Eyes" Santorelli: during the 1990s, he led *The Tanglewood Boys*, a Mafia recruitment gang.

Joseph Lubrano

Capo: Joseph "Big Joe" Lubrano: was arrested on September 11, 2010 on armed robbery charges. He is currently imprisoned with a projected release date of October 31, 2014.

Manhattan & Long Island

Capo: Aniello "Neil" Migliore: was released from prison on May 14, 1997. He served on a *ruling panel* that ran the family from 2003–2009 along with Joseph DiNapoli and Matthew Madonna.

Capo: Dominic "Crazy Dom" Truscello: runs the *Prince Street Crew*. On September 6, 2000, Truscello, Steven Crea and Joseph Tangorra were charged with bid rigging, corrupting construction labor officials among other crimes. In 2003, Truscello plead guilty to extortion. On January 9, 2006, he was released from prison.

Brooklyn faction

Capo: Domenico "Danny" Cutaia: runs the *Brownsville Crew*. On October 25, 2009, he was sentenced to three years in prison for bank fraud. Cutaia was released from prison on October 4, 2013.

Capo: John "Big John" Castelle: runs the *Bensonhurst Crew*. On November 12, 2000 Castelle was charged along with brother underboss Eugene Castelle and others on drug trafficking, extortion and loansharking operations in Bensonhurst, Brooklyn. On October 20, 2004 he was released from prison.

New Jersey faction

Capo: Ralph Vito Perna: runs the New Jersey faction. In December 2007, Peran was arrested along with DiNapoli and Madonna and other members of the New Jersey faction on illegal gambling charges.

Capo: Joseph "Joey" Giampa: was found guilty in August 1995 of conspiring to establish gambling operations and racketeering in New Jersey. On September 21, 2001, Giampa was released from prison.

Historical leadership

Boss (official and acting)

1922–1930: Gaetano "Tommy" Reina: murdered on February 26, 1930

1930: Bonaventura "Joseph" Pinzolo: murdered on September 5, 1930

1930–1951: Tommaso "Tommy" Gagliano: retired in 1951, died on February 16, 1953

1951–1967: Gaetano "Tommy Brown" Lucchese: died on July 13, 1967

Acting 1966–1967: Carmine Tramunti: stepped down

Acting 1967: Ettore "Eddie" Coco: stepped down

1967–1973: Carmine "Mr. Gribbs" Tramunti: imprisoned in October 1973

1973–1986: Anthony "Tony Ducks" Corallo: indicted on February 15, 1985, convicted on November 19, 1986 in the Mafia Commission Trial and sentenced on January 13, 1987 to 100 years in prison.

1986–2009: Vittorio "Vic" Amuso: arrested in 1991, received a life sentence in January 1993

Acting 1990–1991: Alphonse "Little Al" D'Arco: demoted, became a member of a *ruling panel*

Acting 1994–1998: Joseph "Little Joe" DeFede: imprisoned in 1998

Acting 1998–2000: Steven "Wonderboy" Crea: imprisoned on September 6, 2000

Acting 2000–2003: Louis "Louie Bagels" Daidone: imprisoned March 2003, received life sentence in January 2004

2009–present: Steven "Wonderboy" Crea

Street Boss

The Street Boss is considered the go-to-guy for the boss and is responsible to pass on orders to lower ranking members. In some instances a *Ruling panel* (of capos) substituted the Street boss role.

1990–1991: Alphonse "Little Al" D'Arco: promoted to *Acting Boss*

1991: *Ruling panel*: Anthony Baratta, Salvatore Avellino, Frank Lastorino and Alphonse D'Arco: on September 21, 1991, D'Arco became a government witness.

1991–1993: *Ruling panel*: Anthony Baratta, Salvatore Avellino, Steven Crea and Domenico Cutaia

2003–2009: *Ruling panel*: Aniello Migliore, Joseph DiNapoli and Matthew Madonna

Underboss

(Official and acting)

1920–1930: Gaetano "Tommy" Gagliano: promoted to boss

1930–1951: Gaetano "Tommy" Lucchese: promoted to boss

1951–1972: Stefano "Steve" LaSalle: retired

1973–1978: Aniello "Neil" Migliore: resigned

1978–1986: Salvatore "Tom Mix" Santoro Sr.: imprisoned in the Commission Case

1986–1989: Mariano "Mac" Macaluso: retired in 1989

1989–1993: Anthony "Gaspipe" Casso: imprisoned, became government witness in 1993

Acting 1990–1992: Anthony "Bowat" Baratta: imprisoned in June 1992.

1993–2009: Steven "Wonderboy" Crea: served as acting boss 1998–2000; imprisoned 2000–2006

Acting 1998–2000: Eugene "Boopsie" Castelle: imprisoned in November 2000

Consigliere
(Official and acting)

1931–1953: Stefano "Steve" Rondelli: retired

1953–1973: Vincenzo "Vinny" Rao: imprisoned from 1965 to 1970, retired

Acting 1965–1967: Mariano "Mac" Macaluso

Acting 1967–1973: Paul "Paulie" Vario: imprisoned 1974 to 1976

1973–1981: Vincent "Vinnie Beans" Foceri: retired

1981–1986: Christopher "Christie Trick" Furnari: imprisoned in 1986

1986–1987: Ettore "Eddie" Coco: retired

1987–1989: Anthony "Gaspipe" Casso: promoted to underboss

1989–1993: Frank "Big Frank" Lastorino: imprisoned in April 1993

1993–1996: Frank Papagni: imprisoned in September 1996

1996–2002: Louis "Louie Bagels" Daidone: promoted to acting boss in 2000

2002–present: Joseph "Joe C." Caridi: imprisoned 2003—2009

Controlled unions

The Lucchese family has taken over unions across United States. The crime family has extorted money from the unions in blackmail, strong-arming, violence and other matters to keep their control over the market. Similar to the other four crime families of New York City they worked on controlling entire unions. With the mob having control over the union they control the entire market. Bid-rigging allows the mob to get a percentage of the income on the construction deal only allowing certain companies to bid on jobs who pay them first. The mob also allows companies to use non-union workers to work on jobs the companies must give a kickback to the mob. Unions give mob members jobs on the books to show a legitimate source of income. The Mafia members get into high union position and began embezzling money from the job and workers.

Clothes manufacturing - In the Garment District of Manhattan, the Union of Needletrades, Industrial and Textile Employees Locals 10, 23, 24, and 25 were controlled by members of the Lucchese family. Lucchese Associates would extort the businesses and organize strikes. Today some unions still are working for the family.

Kosher meat companies - In the early 1960s Giovanni "Johnny Dio" Dioguardi merged *Consumer Kosher Provisions Company* and *American Kosher Provisions Inc.* together. Dio was able to control a large portion of the Kosher food market, forcing supermarkets to buy from his companies at his prices.

Food distribution - At the Hunts Point Cooperative Market in the Hunts Point section of the Bronx, the

Lucchese family controlled unions involved in the food distribution industry.

Airport services and freight handling - At John F. Kennedy International Airport, LaGuardia and Newark Liberty, the unions were controlled by the Lucchese family.

Construction - Teamsters unions in New York City and New Jersey have been under Lucchese control; Mason Tenders Locals 46, 48, and 66 were controlled by the old Vario Crew.

Newspaper production and delivery - In November 2009, Manhattan District Attorney Robert Morgenthau sent search warrants to investigate the Newspaper Mail Deliverers Union. This union controlled circulation, production and delivery offices at The New York Times, The New York Post, The New York Daily News and El Diario La Prensa. When the Cosa Nostra took control over the union, the price and costs for newspapers increased. Charges were put against many union members as well as the former union President Douglas LaChance. LaChance is accused as being Lucchese crime family associate. In the 1980s LaChance was convicted on labor racketeering charges and served five years in prison. He was also involved in the Manhattan 1990s case were New York Post was being strong-armed into switching their delivery companies, but was acquitted in the case.

Government informants and witnesses

Name Rank and Year

Eugenio Giannini Soldier (1950s)

Henry Hill Associate (1980)

Peter Chiodo Captain (1991)

Alphonse D'Arco Acting Boss (1991)

Joseph D'Arco Soldier (1991)

Anthony Accetturo Captain (1993)

Thomas Ricciardi Soldier (1993)

Frank Suppa Soldier (1993)

Anthony Casso Underboss (1994)

Frank Gioia Jr. Soldier (1994)

Frank Gioia Sr. Soldier (1994)

Joseph DeFede Acting Boss (2002)

Vincent Salanardi Soldier (2004)

Burton Kaplan Associate (2006)

In popular culture

In the 1981 film *Gangster Wars*, Gaetano "Tommy Brown" Lucchese was played by actor Jon Polito.

The 1990 film *Goodfellas* was based on Henry Hill's recollections about his involvement with The Vario Crew of the Lucchese family.

In the 1991 film *Mobsters*, Tommy Reina was played by actor Christopher Penn.

In the 1991 film *Out for Justice*, the William Forsythe character "Richard Madano" was allegedly based on Lucchese mobster Matthew Madonna.

The 1999-2007 HBO TV-show *The Sopranos*, main character Anthony Soprano was based on Lucchese mobster Michael Taccetta.

In 2005 and 2006, a fictionalized version of The Tanglewood Boys was featured on *CSI: NY*, in episode 1.13 "Tanglewood" and in episode 2.20 "Run Silent, Run Deep".

The 2006 film *Find Me Guilty*, was based on the 1980s trial of 20 members of the Lucchese Jersey Crew.

The 2006 Electronic Arts video game *The Godfather: The Game*, the Stracci Family resembles the Lucchese family. In the game, the family is based in New Jersey; the Lucchese family has a large power base in New Jersey.

In the 2007 film *American Gangster*, the Armand Assante character *Dominic Cattano* was allegedly based on Lucchese mobster Carmine Tramunti.

In the 2008 Rockstar North's video game *GTA IV*, the fictional *Lupisella family* resembles on the Lucchese family. The Lupisella family is mainly based in Bohan, the GTA 4 version of the Bronx, and is operating in Liberty City, the game's version of New York City.

Bibliography: The Bonanno Crime Family

Andy. The Bonanno Crime Family: The First Century.

Bonanno, Joseph with Sergio Lalli. *A Man of Honor.* New York: St. Martins Press, 1983.

Capeci, Jerry. The Bonanno Boat Springs a Big Leak. . (3 March 2003).

Capeci, Jerry. Commission Okayed Hits of 3 Capos.(29 January 2004).

Capeci, Jerry. *The Complete Idiots Guide to the Mafia.* Indianapolis: Alpha Books, 2002.

Capeci, Jerry. Dark Days For Joe Massino & Peter Gotti. (21 August 2003).

Capeci, Jerry. Massino Case: Donnie Brasco II. (5 June 2003).

Capeci, Jerry. Turncoat: I Whacked 3 Bonanno Capos. (8 January 2004).

Glaberson, William. From Witness Stand, Tales of Murder and Mob Betrayal. *New York Times,* 29 June 2004. B1.

Glaberson, William. Grisly Crimes Described by Prosecutors as Mob Trial Opens. *New York Times,* 25 May 2004. B1.

Pistone, Joseph D. with Richard Woodley. *Donnie Brasco: My Undercover Life in the Mafia.* New York: Signet, 1987.

Rashbaum, William K. Skeletal Remains Are Believed To Be Those of Mob Captains. *New York Times,* 13 October 2004. B3.

Sifakis, Carl. *The Mafia Encyclopedia.* New York: Checkmark Books, 1999.

Weissenstein, Michael. Feds to Seek Death Penalty for Mobster Joseph Massino. *Associated Press.* (12 November 2004).

Wikipedia

Bibliography The Colombo Family

Andy. The Colombo Crime Family: The First Century. *Gang Land News.*

Capeci, Jerry. The Colombo Family. *New York.* 17 Jan. 2005, p. 29.

Capeci, Jerry. Colombo War Fallout. *Gang Land News.* (18 Nov. 1999).

Capeci, Jerry. *The Complete Idiots Guide to the Mafia.* Indianapolis: Alpha, 2002.

Capeci, Jerry. Like Father, Like Son. *Gang Land News.* (14 Oct. 1999.)

Capeci, Jerry. Mikey Scars Has a Date with Persico. *Gang Land News.* (13 Jan. 2005).

Capeci, Jerry. The Persicos: Father and Son. *Gang Land News.*

Capeci, Jerry. The Shot That Lost the War. *Gang Land News* (6 May 2004).

Sifakis, Carl. *The Mafia Encyclopedia.* New York: Checkmark Books, 1999.

Wikipedia

Bibliography Gambino crime family

Capeci, Jerry. "Gambinos in Free Fall." Gang Land News. 15 July 1999.

Coffey, Joseph and Jerry Schmetterer. *The Coffey Files.* New York, St. Martin 's Press. 1991.

Davis, John. *Mafia Dynasty.* New York, HarperTorch. 1993.

The Gotti Tapes. New York, Times Books. 1992.

Mustain, Gene and Jerry Capeci. *Murder Machine: The True Story of Murder, Madness, and the Mafia.* New York, Dutton. 1992.

O'Brien, Joseph F. and Andrew Kurins. *Boss of Bosses: The Fall of the Godfather—the FBI and Paul Castellano.* New York, Simon and Schuster. 1991.

Sifakis, Carl. *The Mafia Encyclopedia.* New York, Checkmark Books. 1999.

Turkus, Burton B. and Sid Feder. *Murder Inc.: The Story of the Syndicate.* New York, Da Capo. 1992.

Wikipedia

Bibliography Genovese crime family

Capeci, Jerry. *The Complete Idiots Guide to the Mafia.* Indianapolis: Alpha Books, 2002.

Capeci, Jerry. Mario Steps Up for the Chin. *This Week in Gang Land.* 20 May 2004.

Connolly, John. The Mobs Glass House. *New York.* 9 January 1995: 33-35.

Dannen, Fredric. *Hit Men.* New York: Vintage, 1991.

Hoffman, Jan. Genovese Family Counselor Is Convicted of Racketeering. *New York Times.* 26 April 2001.

Maas, Peter. *Underboss: Sammy The Bull Gravano's Story of Life in the Mafia.* New York: HarperCollins, 1997.

Sifakis, Carl. *The Mafia Encyclopedia, Second Edition.* New York: Checkmark Books, 1999.

Tuohy, John William. The Puppet Boss. *Rick Porrellos American Mafia.com.* Nov. 2001.

Wikipedia

Bibliography Lucchese crime family

Andy. "The Lucchese Crime Family: The First Century."

Capeci, Jerry. *The Complete Idiot's Guide to the Mafia.* Indianapolis: Alpha Books, 2002.

Capeci, Jerry. "Daidone's Bird Is Cooked." (29 January 2004).

Capeci, Jerry. "Fat Pete Sits One Out". (7 April 1997).

Capeci, Jerry. "Fearing Future, Little Joe Sings." (7 March 2002).

Capeci, Jerry. "Gangster Goes Down the Sewer." (24 June 1999).

Capeci, Jerry. "Gaspipe's Follies." (20 January 1997).

Capeci, Jerry. "Gaspipe Gets Gassed." (6 July 1998).

Capeci, Jerry. "Gaspipe's Worst Enemy—Gaspipe." (15 September 1997.)

Capeci, Jerry. "Louie Crossbay In Feds' Crosshairs." (25 September 2003.)

Capeci, Jerry. "A Lousy Legacy." (29 August 2002).

Capeci, Jerry. "31 and Counting." (14 December 1998).

Machi, Mario. "New York-New Jersey."

May, Allan. "Alphonse "Little At" D'Arco—Revisited (Part 2)." *Allan May Mob Report.* (11 November 2002).

Sifakis, Carl. *The Mafia Encyclopedia.* New York: Checkmark Books, 1999.

Volkman, Ernest. *Gangbusters: The Destruction of America's Last Great Mafia Dynasty.* New York: Avon. 1999.

Wikipedia

Look for these and other great books
By David Pietras

From "Mommy to Monster"

The "Daddy Dearest" Club

The Manson Family "Then and Now"

When Love Kills

The Making of a Nightmare

THE INFAMOUS "FLORIDA 5"

Death, Murder, and Vampires Real Vampire Stories

The Life and Death of Richard Ramirez, The Night Stalker
(History's Killers Unmasked Series)

Profiling The Killer of a Childhood Beauty Queen

No Justice For Caylee Anthony

A Texas Style Witch Hunt "Justice Denied" The Darlie
Lynn Routier Story by

The Book of Revelations Explained The End Times

Murder of a Childhood

John Gotti: A True Mafia Don (History's Killers Unmasked
Series)

MURDERED FOR HIS MILLIONS The Abraham Shakespeare Case

The Son of Sam "Then and Now" The David Berkowitz Story

A LOOK INSIDE THE FIVE MAFIA FAMILIES OF NEW YORK CITY

Unmasking The Real Hannibal Lecter

Top 10 Most Haunted Places in America

40 minutes in Abbottabad The Raid on Osama bin Laden

In The Footsteps of a Hero The Military Journey of General David H. Petraeus

BATTLEFIELD BENGHAZI

CASE CLOSED The State of Florida vs. George Zimmerman THE TRUTH REVEALED

CROSSING THE THIN BLUE LINE

THE GHOST FROM MY CHILDHOOD A TRUE GHOST STORY ABOUT THE GELSTON CASTLE AND THE GHOST OF "AUNT" HARRIET DOUGLAS...

Haunted United Kingdom

In Search of Jack the Ripper (History's Killers Unmasked Series)

The Last Ride of Bonnie and Clyde

The Meaning of a Tragedy Canada's Serial Killers Revealed

MOMSTER

Murder In The Kingdom

The Shroud of Turin and the Mystery Surrounding Its Authenticity

The Unexplained World That We Live In